"Connie Cavanaugh has a unique ability to share from her heart to your heart. She makes you laugh out loud one moment and wipe tears from your eyes in the next. You don't just read her books; you experience them. You will love this book."

DR. RICHARD BLACKABY
coauthor of *Experiencing God*

"Connie is the gold standard for communicating biblical truths to an audience. She manages to be knee-slapping hilarious yet deep, nuanced, and inspiring. Her material comes straight from her heart, where she stores personal anecdotes that are refreshing, bright, and just so doggone funny that listeners and readers are crying tears of laughter while soaking up her original, intelligent, God-provided wisdom. Time spent with Connie is, quite simply, a blast."

CAROLYN CURTIS
author, journalist, founding editor of
SBC's *On Mission* magazine

"Connie Cavanaugh's book *Following God One Yes at a Time* is a must read for anyone who is ready to step out into a life-changing adventure and trust God. Connie blazes a trail that will help you follow God into His best for your life."

LINDA EVANS SHEPHERD
author of *When You Don't Know How to Pray—
How to Talk to God About Anything*

"Connie Cavanaugh believes that life is a pilgrimage…In this wonderful book she invites you to walk along with her to see how her journey may instruct your own. She isn't bossy concerning what you ought to be learning from her. She is just an agent of grace interpreting her experiences so that you can read her life and apply only those things that might enrich your own. There is much to be learned in this book. Take time for it. Lean into its content. And above all, listen."

CALVIN MILLER
author of *The Singer*

"Connie Cavanaugh packs in brilliant writing, wise advice, and warm wit to create a life-changing book everyone can enjoy and benefit from."

PAM FARREL
international speaker and author of
Men Are Like Waffles, Women Are Like Spaghetti

"Not a day goes by when some aspiring writer doesn't ask me for advice on getting published or show me the next surefire formula for a bestseller we can turn into a mini-series on NBC. Connie was one of those that I'm thankful I didn't laugh at when she humbly showed me her initial idea for a book. Connie's heart for Jesus and for others is so evident, it invades all she does."

PHIL CALLAWAY
author, speaker

"Connie Cavanaugh combines hilarity, transparency, and God-given insights into a package that really delivers."

RHONDA RHEA
radio personality, humor columnist, author of
Whatsoever Things Are Lovely

"Do you long to follow God wherever He wants to take you but the fear of unknown territory holds you back? You can fulfill God's purpose and plans for you, no matter how big they seem. In *Following God One Yes at a Time,* Connie Cavanaugh gives practical advice for overcoming barriers and saying 'yes' to God!"

KATHY HOWARD
author of *Before His Throne*

FOLLOWING GOD

AT A TIME

Connie Cavanaugh

HARVEST HOUSE PUBLISHERS

EUGENE, OREGON

Cover by e210 Design, Eagan, Minnesota

Cover photo © Beata Becla / Shutterstock

FOLLOWING GOD ONE YES AT A TIME
Copyright © 2011 by Connie Cavanaugh
Published by Harvest House Publishers
Eugene, Oregon 97402
www.harvesthousepublishers.com

Library of Congress Cataloging-in-Publication Data
Cavanaugh, Connie.
Following God one yes at a time / Connie Cavanaugh.
p. cm.
ISBN 978-0-7369-3017-8 (pbk.)
1. Spirituality. I. Title.
BV4501.3.C4195 2011
248—dc22

2010035723

Printed in the United States of America

17 18 / VP-SK / 10 9 8 7 6 5 4 3

CONTENTS

To Gerry.
Thank you for living this message and
helping me live it and share it.
Je t'aime.

A Missed Turn

*Do not remember the past events, pay no attention to
things of old. Look, I am about to do something new;
even now it is coming. Do you not see it? Indeed, I will
make a way in the wilderness, rivers in the desert.*

ISAIAH 43:18-19

With the gas pedal pressed close to the floor of my VW Jetta, I hunched over the steering wheel, willing my "folksmobile" to go even faster. But her four-cylinder diesel engine was no match for the hundreds-of-horse-power engine in the 24-foot rental moving truck I'd been chasing for almost 30 minutes. I was slowly gaining ground on the big yellow Ryder truck, but it was taking me a lot longer than I thought it would. I flashed my lights over and over, signaling to the truck driver to pull over, but my husband obviously didn't notice. Perhaps it was the glare of an August afternoon. Or maybe Gerry just wasn't looking in his rearview mirror at the right times. I honked the horn, but with his windows closed, the air-conditioning unit blowing noisily, and the distance between us, I guess he couldn't hear that either. I was going to have to overtake him to get his attention. I jammed the pedal deep into the floorboards and inched forward.

Heading West

Hours earlier Gerry and I had set off to our new life in Alberta, Canada, approximately 4000 kilometers (2500 miles) to the west of

Quebec, where we had lived for four years. We were going to make a little side trip into Northern Saskatchewan to see our extended family, so our total distance would be closer to 5000 kilometers over the next five days. Gerry was driving the truck, fully loaded, and with him was our daughter Christine, age 11, and our son, Jean-Paul, age 3. In the front passenger seat of the Volkswagen I was driving was our 9-year-old middle child, Anita.

We had done the do-it-yourself, two-vehicle moving routine before: going from Saskatchewan to California, and then going from California to the French Canadian province of Quebec. *Neither of those trips were much fun,* I recalled sourly as I tried to catch the Ryder truck hurtling down the highway in front of me. *And the way things are going after just a few hours into this trip, it's obvious this trek isn't going to be a ball of laughs either,* I decided. *At least I'm not pregnant and nauseous this time, as I was on move two. And I don't have two toddlers to manage like I did on move one.* But if Gerry planned to drive like he was on the Autobahn all the way to our new province, I had news for him—and I planned to share it with him if I ever caught up with him.

Follow the Big Yellow Truck

When we started this trip, the plan had been, as per our other moves, for him to lead the way in the truck and for me to follow in the car. We didn't have cell phones back then, and we didn't think walkie-talkies or CB radios were necessary because we'd gotten by without them before. We knew the drill for moving. Gerry planned the trip and, as always, he knew which roads to take. My job was simple: Follow the big yellow truck.

We had regularly scheduled stops to eat, stretch, and swap children. We even had a plan if either of us needed to make an unscheduled stop. It was simple. If Gerry needed to stop the truck, he would pull over and I would follow suit. If I needed to stop, I'd flash my lights or honk. If Gerry didn't notice, I would pull out, pass him, and then pull over. He would follow suit.

But now I knew the hitch in our plan. I couldn't pass a truck I couldn't catch. And the honking and flashing was about as noticeable as a mother's voice to a teen wearing ear buds with the iPod volume cranked to the max.

A New Plan

Gerry and I had already rewritten the rules once in the first few hours. After going 30 miles or so, Gerry was anxious because he couldn't see me in his rearview mirror. Being a more aggressive driver, he passed cars often, so several vehicles had stacked up between us.

So he quit passing cars and drove at my pace. But then the cars piled up behind me, the drivers got frustrated and took crazy chances to pass me, and then they ended up trapped between me and the big truck.

Frustrated at our slow progress, Gerry finally pulled over. I followed. We talked and made a new plan. I would lead, and he would follow. "I can't see your little car in my rearview mirror but you will easily be able to see my big yellow truck in yours," he assured me.

We got back onto the highway with me in the lead. I'd been "advised" to go a little faster, and I was determined to comply. But if you've ever driven a VW Jetta, circa 1987, you know that top speed—downhill with a tail wind—is about 50 miles per hour. And there was one other little factor we'd not discussed when I took the lead. I didn't know where we were going. Well, I knew where we were supposed to end up, but I didn't know the route Gerry had planned. And he had the map and itinerary with him. My job had been to follow, but now I was in the lead.

If you're familiar with Canada, you know that if you head north out of Montreal hoping to get to Calgary, Alberta, at some point you have to go west by turning left.

Sure enough, we hadn't gone very far with me in the lead when the road signs indicated a sharp left turn for a major exit ahead. I sailed right on by the turnoff because I thought we were heading west already. I sped on, oblivious to my error because I was focused on one thing: speed! I was gunnin' for bear…unfortunately it was polar bear.

One Missed Turn

Gerry saw the signs for the left turn coming up and slowed down, believing I would notice him falling back. I didn't. He flashed his lights. No response from me. He honked. I kept on going. Finally, not knowing what else to do, he took the turn, hoping I would see the large, bright-yellow truck turning. No such luck. I disappeared over a hill in a black cloud of diesel exhaust and was gone. He pulled over and waited, sure that I would quickly notice his absence and turn back.

I went down the highway another 15 miles before glancing in my mirror to check on Gerry's progress. When I didn't see the truck, my first thought wasn't alarm. I was smugly satisfied that I had set such a lively pace he couldn't keep up. Ha! Having just come over a big hill, I pulled off onto a farmyard approach and angled my car so I could see the road behind me. I waited, expecting to see him come over the hill at any moment. Since the traffic volume had dropped way down and the road size had mysteriously diminished to a country road with no shoulders, I figured Gerry could lead again. That's what I planned to tell him when he pulled over to congratulate me on my speedy progress.

When 15 minutes passed, I got a bit anxious. I grew alarmed when another 10 minutes passed, and he didn't show up. I decided to retrace my route to see if he'd had engine trouble or a flat tire. Those were the only reasons I could think of that would delay him. Just then I saw a big yellow truck crest the top of the hill and come barreling down. Even though he could clearly see me stopped on the side of the road, Gerry went by me so fast he almost peeled the paint off my car.

So that's the way you wanna play, eh? I thought as my competitive juices kicked in. I slammed my car into gear and took off after him. He'd obviously decided to take the lead and assumed I would get the hint when he *flew* by. I gunned the motor but I didn't gain on him. He was really moving! I flew over bumps and bounced around potholes in my little Jetta. Anita laughed at the tummy tickles, hollering "Whee!"

Oops!

After 30 minutes of pushing the folksmobile to almost impossible limits, I managed to get close to the Ryder truck. I flashed the car lights and honked the horn, but the moving van didn't stop. I finally came to a place where I could pass safely. Signaling, I pulled into the oncoming lane and inched forward. Coaxing every bit of muscle out of the over-taxed car, I pulled up even with the driver's window of the Ryder truck. Anita rolled down her window and looked up, ready to wave and smile. Instead she shrieked, "That's not Daddy!" Before she could get her window shut she heard some "schoolyard French" from the driver of the truck. He was angry—probably from trying to outrun a maniac female driver.

As I hit the brakes and fell back, my heart was thudding and my brain was fuzzy. I pulled over and spent a few minutes calming my distraught daughter, who bemoaned her French fluency that had allowed her to understand the truck driver's colorful language. Pretty shaken up myself, I realized I must have missed a turn but Gerry hadn't.

I turned back and retraced my route. When I got to the major exit, this time I paid attention to the signs and realized this was probably the turn I'd skipped. After making the right turn, it wasn't long before I found Gerry. I could tell he'd been almost crazy with worry, but now there was only relief in his eyes when we finally arrived with an overheated engine.

After wiping away the tears, we spent several minutes carefully outlining a new plan. Gerry explained "where to go and how to get there" (in a good way) and what to do in case we got separated again. We got back into our vehicles. He led and I followed. I stuck so close I probably saved a fortune on fuel by drafting (avoiding wind resistance via the truck's massive size). Without mishap but with calloused hands from gripping the steering wheel, I pulled into the driveway of our new address five days later.

Following: How Hard Can It Be?

What I discovered in trying to follow that big yellow truck has proven true in my life as a Christ-follower too. Even though God and I started out together, somehow I lost my way. When I met Jesus as a teen and He said, "Follow Me," I thought obeying was the simplest thing in the world. Jesus leads; I follow. Duck soup.

A few months after establishing a personal relationship with Jesus, I was completely baffled when my college roommate, a young woman who had been following Jesus since she was a child, expressed doubt and fear as she wept over her struggle to continue believing in Jesus. Still in my honeymoon of faith, I had no comprehension of what she was dealing with. "Just follow Jesus," I told her over and over. It was so simple. Jesus leads; we follow.

Today I look back on that time with so much empathy and understanding for my roomie's spiritual struggle. Having endured 10 years of spiritual dryness, I now know what being off track is like. I lost my way so profoundly that I suspected I'd been duped by this "personal God" who was supposed to know and love me. I decided the whole Jesus thing was an invention of the evangelical church. *If there is a God,* I figured, *He's nothing more than an "intelligent designer" who set the world spinning and allowed life on earth to evolve without His direct involvement.*

How did I miss the turns God had mapped out for me? Why did I get so far off course? And how did I find my way back to God? After so many years of wandering, I wondered, *Will God still let me help Him? Will He allow me to assist in furthering His kingdom and plans?*

Faith for the Real World

My book *From Faking It to Finding Grace* explains my meandering trail through the wilderness and what those years felt like. I was married to a Canadian pastor active in a national Christian ministry and I wrote articles, and columns on the Christian life. And yet I had profoundly but secretly lost my way. But God continued to pursue me, and I finally found Him in the midst of the dryness. Yes by yes I simultaneously followed Him back *into* His presence and *out* to a hurting world.

This book, *Following God One Yes at a Time,* is an encouraging, upbeat guide that maps out how you can ignite (or reignite) your faith. Whether you are "on the far side of the wilderness" like Moses was when God lit his world on fire with a flaming bush to get his attention or you occasionally lose sight of your heavenly Leader and fear you are losing your way, the principles in this book will help you get moving forward. They will also help you reduce the threat of spiritual dryness in the future.

From Faking It to Finding Grace tells the story of becoming lost but being pursued—and found!—by God. *Following God One Yes at a Time* reveals what we can do in response to His loving pursuit.

Shared Secrets

Speaking to thousands of people during the past 10 years has let me in on a little secret many Christians hold on to pretty tightly. By publicly admitting my wilderness journey, I opened the door for others to share their experiences. And guess what? This group is much larger than I imagined. Countless times after telling my story listeners came forward to meet me, eager to tell *their* stories of dryness and confess in whispers, "Somewhere along the way I lost my faith, and I don't know where to find it. I never dreamed this would happen to me. I don't know how much longer I can fake it. Can you help me?"

You will meet some of them in these pages. Their stories will give you courage and hope.

Is This Book for Me?

Maybe you are like I was the day I missed that turn west when driving across Canada. You thought you knew where you were going, but eventually you realized you weren't paying attention and must have missed something. Or perhaps you got out in front of God when He wanted you to follow Him but stick a little closer. You could be chasing the wrong leader, believing he's the one but realizing something isn't quite right. Then again, perhaps you've realized you're off course or you're backtracking, in search of the Leader you once followed...but you're not sure where you two parted ways.

How can something so simple as Jesus' command to "follow Me" get so complicated? If you want to know and want to get back on track, this book is for you. This book is also for you if...

- your faith has run dry and you don't know what to do.
- your walk with God has become too complicated, and you want to get back to the basics of living for Him.
- you've lost hope because you keep trying to follow God but you always mess up.

- you are so comfortable in your life that the stillness is starting to get to you. You know there's more to following Jesus
  but you're a little scared of what He might want you to
  give.

- you feel apathetic, like you're going through the motions.
  Cynicism has set in. You question whether following God
  is worthwhile. You've "been there, done that" and aren't
  satisfied.

- the life you want seems so out of reach. You want to experience God now. You want to be sure you're on the right
  road and following an accurate map.

- you're floating around aimlessly, wondering what to do
  with your life. You lack dreams or you feel pursuing the
  dreams you have is useless.

- you feel stuck—and have felt that way for a long time. You
  need a push or pull to help you get moving.

- you're not sure you believe in a God who wants a personal
  relationship with you, knows you, cares about you, and
  has a plan for you.

- you want to more fully see Him, hear Him, sense Him,
  love Him, follow Him, serve Him.

Following God in the Real World

Not everyone who starts out following God will go through a wilderness, but the Israelites did—and I did too. The wilderness was where
we developed faith *strong* enough (not *big* enough—faith isn't a matter of size) to fight the battles ahead. The wilderness forced me out of
childish theology and into *childlike following.* Coming out of the wilderness *one yes at a time* taught me how to follow God in a workable,
real-world way. Following Him requires the simple trust and immediate obedience of a child who believes God will make the way to Him
simple, immediate, and *possible.* These three principles guided me back
to God—and into a new life.

Beneath His overarching purpose for my life—to know Him and make Him known, becoming more like Him, and making a difference for good in the world—are many overlapping dreams we pursue together. *He* gives the dreams (I don't just dream them up and ask Him to bless them). Then He helps me move forward so I can realize the dreams He plants in my heart. Pursuing the dreams often leads through enemy territory. During those times God and I, together, confront and overcome barriers, such as fear, pride, guilt, shame, comparison, and doubt, that try to keep me locked up, defeated, and ineffective for God. En route to attaining my dreams, God strategically places little "chocolates on the trail." These markers occur every time I sense His presence, feel His peace, see His power, and recognize His provision. They are reminders that God is real, that He loves me, and that I am on His path—the right path.

The adult companions to childlike faith are realistic expectations of life in a sin-riddled world, battle-hardened resolve, belief that God *is* love regardless of circumstance, and openness to spiritual interaction that defies logic. These are the basic foundations upon which Christ followers tread as they *follow God one yes at a time* through terrain that is unfamiliar, steep, rocky, and occasionally shrouded in dense fog.

Are you up for the adventure? I hope so! We're about to go on an incredible journey together as we discover more about living for Christ.

The Dream

*The Lord is my rock, my fortress,
and my deliverer, my God.*

Psalm 18:2

Oblivious to the late-summer sun warming his back, Gerry hunched, unmoving, atop a huge rock on the hillside below our home, head in hands, elbows on knees, legs in the lotus position. The rock lay like a sleeping buffalo on the hillside, making it a perfect refuge for respite from the demands of the telephone, two toddlers, and me. Mostly me. I had an endless honey-do list.

Gerry didn't discover this rock until after the big grassfire. Prior to the blaze, brome grass, buck brush, chokecherry, and pin cherry bushes, along with an accumulated pile of junk previous tenants had stashed out there made the area an eyesore. The fire was Gerry's solution to my nagging to clean up the unsightly mess. We got the idea for the burn from a neighbor who had torched his backyard in the spring to clear brush and debris and make a place for a lawn. The grass started growing within a few weeks! His fire fizzled out in puffs of steamy smoke in the spring snow banked beneath the wire fence around his yard.

"Just burn the hillside," I suggested innocently.

Gerry agreed, but he was a busy man. Weeks passed. It was the hottest, driest spring on record. In mid-June, Gerry decided to surprise me with a tidy hillside. After I left for work, he ran a line of gasoline along the top edge of the hill and casually tossed a lit match toward the soaked grass.

Kaboom! The fire took off in every direction. Gerry stomped out the flames galloping toward our house and then noticed that just in front of our walkout basement a carpet was smoldering because it was draped over four flaming sawhorses. Our water heater had boiled over the week before, flooding the basement, and Gerry had manhandled the sodden rug out to the sunny little plateau to dry. He yanked the carpet away from the burning sawhorses and jumped up and down on it, trying to put out the flames. As he was doing that, the grassfire gained momentum and headed down the two-acre hillside.

The carpet fire put out, Gerry hooked up the hose to control the grassfire, but the hottest part of the fire was already beyond its water-squirting reach. From inside the house he grabbed a small throw rug and a plastic garbage can. Dashing back outside, he filled the pail and soaked the rug so he could beat back the flames. No sooner did he subdue the blaze in one area then he would dash off to take on the flames somewhere else. He was horrified by the size and fury of the fiery beast that was creating its own wind. He said it felt like a blast furnace.

Gerry realized he needed help. Running to the scattered homes of our nearest neighbors, he frantically pounded on doors, yelling, "There's a fire! It's coming your way!"

The Nonvoluntary Ladies Fire Brigade

The only people home at that time of day were four elderly women. They grabbed rakes, hoses, and gunnysacks, and came running, aprons flapping over their housedresses. Connecting their hoses to make a longer hose line, they filled their pails and, sloshing water, lugged them to the most threatening sections.

They stomped their oversized rubber boots.

They flailed sodden sacks.

They raked the embers into piles and poured water on them.

Inch by inch they beat back the flames, hoping to stop the fire before it consumed the holiday cottages nestled among the overhanging poplars and aspens along the lakeshore.

"I don't think we're gonna get it out," Gerry gasped, chest heaving as he filled his pail.

"Oh we're gonna get it out, all right!" shouted our usually good-natured neighbor Florence. "Or you'll be sorry!"

Gerry dove in with renewed vigor.

Hours later, when the old gals were satisfied the fire was out and had little chance of reigniting, they gathered at the large rock where Gerry had slumped after putting out the last tendril of fire. Circling him, they made sure he understood what his job was for the remainder of that day: to keep a sharp lookout and quench even the tiniest puff of smoke. "Or else!" they added. (The locals now joke that Gerry is the minister who put the word "arson" in parson.)

Surprise, Surprise!

Late that afternoon I got off the bus on the highway in front of our church and walked down the 100-yard gravel driveway toward home. I couldn't see the denuded hillside from the driveway, but I was puzzled by a hint of smoke in the air. When I stepped inside the house and saw a trail of sooty water across the white linoleum, my kitchen throw rug in a soggy, blackened pile, and the scorched carbuncular blob that once had been my garbage can, I knew something was amiss. Looking for answers, I went back outside. Florence was striding across our lawn, coming toward me. She hailed me with, "What is it with Baptist preachers and fire? The last guy did the same dang thing!" Florence's sense of humor was back as she howled at her own joke. Refreshed by a hot shower and a stiff drink, her eyes danced in her weathered face. Seeing the look of confusion on my face, she simply pointed to the edge of the hill. "Your husband is down there, and he's probably hungry." I rushed to the lip of the hill and gasped. Our entire two acres was blackened, with charcoal peninsulas snaking onto the neighboring properties as well.

Seeing me atop the hill gave Gerry a saved-by-the-cavalry-feeling after several solitary hours at his post. I minced my way downhill in my high heels and ivory pantsuit. Blacker than a chimney sweep, Gerry sat atop the rock clutching the burned off end of a dribbling hose that had so many small geysers along its length that little pressure remained. After glancing at me briefly, his reddened eyes darted to and fro in search of smoke. Deadly earnest, he told me how he had saved our home and then, together with his valiant crew, the lakeside cottages and possibly the town.

After listening to his story, I headed back up the hill and into the kitchen to fix Gerry a sandwich. When I got there, the dam burst and I laughed until I cried.

Sitting on the Rock

Gerry had had more time than usual to think that day because he was pinned to the "lookout" rock until sundown. From that point on the rock became his place to retreat to when he needed to think and pray. This was where three years and two babies later God gave him a dream.

"Finish your education," He said.

"What! Now? I have a wife and two kids to support!" Gerry responded. "And things are just getting going in the church. Why would I leave now?"

"Follow Me."

"But how am I going to do it?"

"I'll be your rock. I'll go with you."

Gerry lacked one year to earning his bachelor's degree. And he dreamed of attaining a master's in ministry. His education had been interrupted a year after the grassfire when our first baby came along and I swapped my teacher's briefcase for a diaper bag. Our tiny church could barely handle the upkeep on the building, much less pay for a pastor, so Gerry worked two part-time jobs. He drove a school bus on weekdays and helped the local butcher on Saturdays. (The first time he cut up a beef hind quarter without supervision, his boss yelled, "I said butcher it, not massacre it!")

Now God gave Gerry a dream: finish the education he had started several years before. But the closest affiliated seminary was 1200 miles away and located in the United States, where there was little opportunity for legal employment for foreign students. We had no savings. We had two preschoolers I was staying home to raise. Gerry and I were both nearing 30, so we were way past the age where our parents would pitch in and help us financially.

The timing was all wrong. The process looked complicated. The dream seemed impossible. With all our hearts we wanted to follow God, but we felt like we were facing a runaway grassfire without a hose, bucket, sack, or help. We wondered, *Where would we even begin?*

A Purpose, a Promise, a Plan

Can you relate? Have you had your own "rock" encounter with God? Did He plant a dream in your heart that you had no idea how to achieve? Have you ever sensed Him urging you to further your education, change careers, move to a faraway place, write a book, make a film, end a destructive relationship, kick a habit, change jobs, improve your marriage, graciously adapt to a new and unwanted status, update your professional skills, be a more effective parent, care for an aging relative, love a difficult child, adopt a healthier lifestyle, accept a circumstance you hate but can't change? What is God challenging you to do right now in your life? How have you responded to Him in the past? How will you respond now?

When God gives us dreams, He has a purpose, a promise, and a plan!

God's purpose is identical for every believer: to make us more like Christ as we follow Him. He will never ask us to do anything that does not lead to our growth in godliness and increased goodness for others:

> "For I know the plans I have for you"—this is the LORD's declaration—"plans for your welfare, not for disaster, to give you a future and a hope" (Jeremiah 29:11).

> We know that all things work together for the good of those who love God: those who are called according to His purpose (Romans 8:28).

His promise is to take us (be with us) as we follow the dreams He gives us. Right after God tells Moses, "Go. I am *sending* you to Pharaoh,"[1] He adds, "I will certainly *be with you.*"[2] He even tells Moses, "I will help you speak and I will teach you what to say."[3] How's that for a hands-on approach?

Jesus restated God's message in His own way when He told the disciples, "My sheep hear My voice, I know them, and they follow Me. I give them eternal life, and they will never perish—ever! No one will snatch them out of My hand."[4] We pursue our dreams hand-in-hand with God—He promises!

His plan is unique to every believer: He calls us as we are to use what we have as we follow Him step-by-step. Every believer is different so our pathways will not be identical. If fulfilling the dream will require more than we have to give at the outset, God will lead us step-by-step to acquire what is needed along the way. We start by utilizing the gifts, talents, abilities, and interests He has already created within us or led us to develop. In other words, the instant He places His dream in your heart, you are ready to go. Nothing is holding you back from saying yes.

> We are His creation—created in Christ Jesus for good works, which God prepared ahead of time so that we should walk in them (Ephesians 2:10).

> He who started a good work in you will carry it on to completion until the day of Christ Jesus (Philippians 1:6).

The Dream Is a Picture-promise

A good way to think of the dream is as a picture-promise. For instance, most people who want to lose weight have a picture in their mind that motivates them. Some add "lost" pounds of butter to a stack in their refrigerator to visually represent their progress. Some blowup an old photo of themselves when they were at their goal weight and tack it to the refrigerator. I even know some women who constructed a fake woman with the pounds they lost and tried to make her as fat as possible. They named her Tiffany and kept a running tab on how big she was. Last time I checked Tiff was nearing 300 pounds.

A picture-promise is the vision of our dream that is ever before us as we move forward. When God promised Abraham he would be the father of nations, God told him to picture his descendants as numerous as the stars in the sky, the sand on the seashore, and the dust in the air.[5] When God promised Moses He would help him free the Israelites from bondage, He gave him a picture of where they were headed: a land flowing with milk and honey[6]—a place where walled cities were already built and vineyards were already in production.

God gives us picture-promises too, which we adopt as our dreams the minute we say yes.

Spiritual Stretch Marks

God did not give me a dream to run marathons, do accounting, develop marketing strategies, invent games, design software, or work in retail. How do I know? I'm not good at those pursuits. I don't have the gifts or interests needed for them. That's not to say that a small portion of my life doesn't involve doing some of those things. As I pursue the dream of being a speaker and writer, I do have to do some things outside my interests, such as keeping financial records, selling products, and marketing.

God stretches us so that we grow. He will lead us into areas that will complement or enhance our main goals. We may be led to accomplish things that might surprise us and those who know us. He personalizes His plan for our lives. And He goes along with us every step of the way to guide, encourage, help, teach, stretch, and correct us.

When God gave me the dreams to be a writer and a speaker, I said yes and began following Him one yes at a time. It wasn't easy. The first time I had to travel to complete a writing assignment, I was so terrified to stay alone in a hotel room that I contacted some old friends and asked if they would let me stay in their home instead. That meant I had to rent a car and drive an hour each way to get to my assignment each day instead of simply walking across the street from the nearest hotel. The first time I was given a magazine cover story, my submission was so awful the editor had to start all over and write it herself at the eleventh hour because she couldn't use what I submitted. The first time I gave a talk at a luncheon I was supposed to speak for 20 minutes and I talked for an hour and a half.

Since those shaky beginnings, God has molded and shaped, refined and revamped, removed and improved, nipped and tucked (I wish He did facelifts!) so that He could use me to make a positive difference in the world I live in. God takes us as we are and makes us into what we need to be to realize His purposes (our dreams).

Are you wondering what kind of dreams God gives? Or how to know if a dream is from Him? Are you worried He'll give you a dream you don't want? Let's cover a few basic principles before we dive in.

God Gives the Dreams

God pursues His children. *He* comes after *us*. He always has. That is a pattern established in Scripture. Before the birth of the Christ, God manifested Himself in many ways—messenger angels, a flaming bush, and a pillar of fire to name a few. He also spoke through His prophets. Then He sent His Son Jesus, who walked and talked and lived among mankind while teaching God's ways. Today we have the Bible and the Holy Spirit to communicate God's truths to us. God wants us to know His plans just as much (or more) than we want to know them! So we need not fret about being left in the dark. Instead, we need to focus on *actively listening* and *earnestly seeking Him*.

Actively Listen; Earnestly Seek

A listener-seeker has a certain position, placement, and posture. Your position with God is that He is God and you are not. That may seem obvious. He knows everything; you do not. He loves you more than you love yourself. He sees your eternal future; you see only the immediate future. He knows what surprises are around the next corner; you are caught by surprise.

You are ready to hear from God when you understand you are the clay and He is the Potter. Then you place your clay pot where He is most likely to fill it. What does that look like? If you were a hunter and you wanted to bag a moose, where would you go to find it? Manhattan or Alaska? In the same way, if you want to hear from God, place yourself where you're most likely to encounter Him. Get into the Bible. Join a church. Find a mentor. Make friends with believers who are accustomed to hearing from God. Tune in to Christian speakers and scholars on the radio, television, and Internet.

Finally, I encourage you to adopt the posture of being a keen learner. Listen eagerly. Show up early. Take notes. Ask questions. Do extra reading. Lean in close. Pay attention. "If you seek Him, He will be found by you."[7]

Don't Jump the Gun

Every dream has its own timeline, so wait for the starter pistol. Ecclesiastes 3:1 says, "There is an occasion for everything, and a time for every activity under heaven." David was anointed king, but it took many years and time on the run from King Saul before David wore the crown that was rightfully his (1 Samuel 16–31).

One of the hardest activities for us to do is wait. Sometimes waiting is part of the plan. Once we know the dream, we want to go after it. Remember, God holds the starter pistol. Don't jump the gun. Watch and wait. My dream to be a writer (God's purpose for me) began in my 20s or maybe even sooner. I wasn't a published author until I was in my 40s. Why? Lots of reasons, but the main one was because other dreams required my immediate and focused attention: marriage, ministry, and maternity. I married a pastor and had two babies within three years.

Let God Be the Judge

You're ready to move toward the dream when God says so. Even though you may think you are qualified, equipped, and available, God may ask you to wait. Conversely, when you may think you're unqualified, ill-equipped, or too busy, God may urge you forward immediately. The timing is not up to us.

I met a woman several years ago who introduced herself as a Christian speaker. She had a prayer team, a focus group, and a fulltime assistant. Her teaching materials were researched and sorted into three-ring binders. She could give a keynote address or present a weekend retreat on a variety of topics. She had a glossy promotional package, complete with DVDs of her teachings that had been widely distributed. She was impressive, and she was ready to get to work. But her calendar was empty. For reasons only God knew, she was in waiting mode. I know of other speakers with full calendars who jot down what they're going to talk about while on the airplane traveling to the event. God's timing can be a mystery to us. He says, "My thoughts are not your thoughts, and your ways are not My ways" (Isaiah 55:8).

Do You Have Dreams?

Perhaps you sense God wants to take you somewhere or put something new into your life. Maybe you believe He wants you to be different in some way. Or perhaps He wants to give you hope where you lacked hope before. Each of these scenarios can be a template for your dreams. Is your lifelong dream to become a physician so you can devote your life to healing? Perhaps your dream is to homeschool your child so he or she can realize his or her full potential. Or maybe you have a short-term dream of fitting into that perfect little black dress…oops… I meant to say "a short-term dream of adopting healthier eating habits." Each dream will have its own requirements, time span, and difficulties before it can be accomplished.

God gave Moses the dream to lead the Israelites (His chosen people) *to* the Promised Land. God gave Joshua the dream to lead the people to enter and *take* the Promised Land. The apostle Paul's dream was to bring the Good News of the gospel of Jesus Christ to the Gentiles. These huge, long-term dreams could only be realized one way—by following God one yes at a time. None of these dreams could be attained without God's involvement. And the same is true for us. Our dreams won't be fulfilled without our Creator God coming alongside *to make something out of the gifts, talents, and opportunities He's given us. And He will do so only* when the time is right.

Barriers to Saying Yes

Have you been given a dream and then confronted thoughts such as these that hold us back from climbing off the rock?

- This dream is too big, and I don't have what it takes.
- The process looks so complicated I'm not sure where to start.
- The finish line is so far away. I don't think I can go the distance.

- I've tried before and dropped out, so I'm all out of chances.

- Is this God speaking or just wishful thinking on my part?

- People like me don't get to do these things. I'm not worthy.

The vast majority of the time, the barriers that keep us from saying yes to God aren't other people or circumstances or even lack of opportunity. No, they exist entirely inside our own heads. We let fear hold us back: This is too big, too complicated, too long-term. Guilt can step in: I should be able to do this…but I'm so scared. Shame muscles to the front and says, "I've messed up royally in the past and done so many things I regret. I don't deserve anything good from God." And along comes the weight of comparison (a subtle form of passing the buck): "Surely others are better suited for this than I am. I'll let them do it. They'll do a better job." And let's not forget about pride: This dream is not big enough. I'm made for a bigger "stage" than this! And last but not least, the icing on the cake is doubt: "How do I even know this is God speaking? Maybe I dreamed this up by myself. Am I deluding myself into thinking God could or would use me in a significant way?"

Gerry experienced some of these barriers as he sat on that rock and tried to absorb the enormity of the dream God had given him. Investing five years to complete the education he'd put on hold twice already seemed unreachable. And adding in the smaller income and more family responsibilities, the dream became ludicrous. Undoable. Impossible. Cue the runaway grassfire. And yet the dream was there. And God was saying, "I will be your rock wherever you go" (Psalm 18:2).

Because he'd started and quit before, Gerry didn't know how he could go back to school now. How was this time going to be any different? He worried he wouldn't make it to the finish. He wondered if he had what it took to be a successful student. And how could he be sure this was God's dream and not his own desire to move on.

Armed with little more than God's promise to go with him, Gerry said yes to following God, yes to accepting by faith that the dream was from Him, and yes to climbing down from the rock and getting started.

How Much Faith Does It Take?

After our family had moved from Saskatchewan to California and then to Quebec and on to Alberta, I met an old friend. I caught him up on the goings on of the last several years and the dreams God had given Gerry and me. I shared how we were following Him one yes at a time and moving forward. The friend, knowing the facts of how *small* we were in comparison to the size of our dreams (that God had given us), said, "I'm amazed at your faith! I never would have had the faith to do the things you've done or go to the places you've gone."

But he was wrong. We didn't have any more faith than he did or than you have. *We all have enough faith to do what God asks us to do.* The way we became believers was *by faith* (Romans 5:1; Ephesians 2:8; Philippians 3:9). At the moment of conversion most of us didn't think we had much faith. But God is sufficient. He enabled us to say yes to Him then. And when we stare into the face of the dreams God gives us, we often question whether our faith is big enough to meet the challenge. It is…in Him!

Well-fed Faith

So how much faith does it take to say yes to God's dream? That's the wrong question. It's not how much faith you have, it's *what kind of faith* you have. Your faith needs to be well-fed. A couple we know spent 15 years in northern Nigeria. The husband and wife are both tall, and their children inherited that trait. Even as youngsters they quickly sprouted up. Their Fulani neighbors were also tall, but they often remarked on the more robust physiques of our friends' kids in comparison to their own. The truth is that our friends' children were healthier and stronger because they ate well. Part of the Fulani culture, dating back centuries, is not to "waste" food on toddlers since many of them die early. So the Fulani's feed them just enough to survive. One of the results is that the growth of many of the children is affected. It's not until they are old enough and strong enough to claim bigger portions of the food supply for themselves that they become healthier.

The same is true for our faith. We will have stunted faith if we don't feed it well. What is well-fed faith? First let me say what it's not.

Well-fed faith *is not* the by-product of being a passive recipient of preaching or having access to top-notch Christian programs. We've all heard people say they left their former churches in search of better ones because they weren't "getting fed." Granted, not all preachers are gifted orators, but even clumsy speakers can deliver God's truths. And, yes, not all churches offer a broad range of programs that span the cradle to the grave, but smaller faith communities provide ample opportunities for involvement at every level if people are willing to serve. Faith doesn't grow by listening to what others say about *how God works*.

Faith does not get fed by what it takes in; faith gets fed by what it puts out (James 1:22-25). A lot of Christians with stunted faith blame their condition on poor preaching, uninspired teaching, or lack of access to Christian programs. What they really need to do is take responsibility for developing their faith by talking to God. We can ask, "God, what do You want me to *do* with and for You?" Faith grows by *getting involved* where God is at work. Because faith grows like a muscle, it needs to be exercised, to be used. And have you noticed that it makes no difference what you feed your muscles, whether hamburger or filet mignon? If you use it, it will grow. "Use it or lose it," fitness buffs say. Faith buffs need to say the same thing. Faith that never gets used is stunted and will become shriveled and useless.

How much faith does it take to say yes to God and get off the rock of contemplation? If you are a child of God, it takes no more than what you already have. A more important question is, What kind of faith does it take to say yes to God and get moving? The answer? The kind of faith that is willing to be used. The kind of faith that may be weak but is willing to grow. Paul said, "When I am weak, then I am strong" (2 Corinthians 12:10). The only way to get your faith growing is to say yes to God and get off the rock. Saying yes *is the first step* to getting off the rock!

Once we get moving, what do we do? Take it one *simple, immediate, possible* yes at a time. We'll get into the meaning of those three adjectives as we go along, but let me illustrate what I mean in reference to getting off the rock. By the time our girls were ready to start school, Gerry only had one more year remaining to complete his master's degree. As the summer approached before his final year of studies,

I sensed God nudging me to pursue a teaching position to improve our financial standing...well, our "financial kneeling." Trying to get a professional job using a degree from another country can be very complicated. (I think that's why doctors and engineers from other countries drive taxis in the United States.) The more I looked into getting a teaching job in the States, the more impossible it seemed. I gathered enough information to conclude it was too complex to even know where to start. As I prayed and actively listened for God's voice, a picture of my husband's secretary's face came to mind. Gerry was pastoring a church in California while getting his degree. His part-time secretary, Louise, was a retired California schoolteacher as well as a very organized thinker. "Call Louise!"

I contacted Louise and invited her for tea. She sat down at my kitchen table that was covered with teaching papers, information, and forms. I told her I wanted to get a teaching job in California and was hoping she could help me. Within the hour Louise laid out a step-by-step approach, showing me what needed to be done and in what order. With her help, I went from an "impossible dream" in June to employed in September.

What had I done? I said yes to the dream and followed God, taking each step only as it became clear. And when I was stalled and didn't know what to do next, I asked God and He brought to my mind someone who was able to get me on track. Even though the dream seemed huge and complicated and impossible, God used Louise to map out the steps I could take each day to realize the dream—a fulltime teaching position.

Following God doesn't have to be complicated. In fact, God doesn't intend it to be a mystery. All of us can pursue His dreams for our lives if we follow Him one yes at a time. Achieving the dreams He gives is *always* possible, no matter how impossible it may seem. Even if you've never done anything like what your dream is, you don't know where to begin, you're too scared to try, you don't think you have what it takes, you have tried and failed so many times you think you've run out of chances, you aren't sure if the voice you heard is God's, you *can* get off the rock by saying one *simple, immediate, possible yes* at a time.

PART I

One Yes
at a Time

2

SIMPLE

Religion is man's effort to reach God. True Christianity is God coming to man in a personal relationship.[1]

BILLY GRAHAM

Gerry has always loved the science of farming, even though he didn't grow up on a farm. Me? Not so much. However, I do prefer the science of farming to the smell of farming. Gerry had access to some land surrounding the church and parsonage of his first pastorate. Having promised the "Ladies Fire Brigade" he would never attempt another burn, he went looking for a safer way to control the overgrowth on our place. Sheep can crop a yard so it looks like a golf green, he discovered. For someone who disliked reading as much as he did, I should have been suspicious when he got a library card. Sure enough, he brought home *Raising Sheep the Modern Way*. He justified the foray into mutton as a nonpyrotechnic solution to our overgrown hillside. "Not to mention free fertilizer!" he exclaimed.

The Grass Is Always Greener

The most abundant source of grass for miles around was in our sheep enclosure, but sheep, like humans, have an eye for the greener side of the fence—even when it's not greener. No sooner did we get a little flock of seven pregnant ewes ("Two for the price of one!") penned in on our property when they found an escape route, bolted across the busy highway, and headed straight for Pete's place. Pete was a Metis[2] trapper who lived on wild meat and bannock, a thick cakey bread.[3] He'd never touched a salad in his life. Pete had neither a garden nor a blade of grass on the dusty hillside he and his family had been living on for decades. Pete's wife, Della, was our most faithful church member, but the only time, other than his wedding day, that Pete showed up for church was the Sunday he came dashing in halfway through the service hollering, "Them dumb sheep are out again, pastor!"

All the men—all four of them—and the older kids jumped out of their seats and ran for the door. This was a lot more fun than singing "I Surrender All" just before the offering plate was passed. Gerry led the charge in his suit and tie, skidding and sliding in his smooth-soled leather loafers. He was, in every sense of the word, a shepherd, that day, as he led one flock in pursuit of another.

One poor ewe, the Houdini of herbivores, escaped so often and ran so hard she developed a perpetual asthmatic wheeze from the exertion and was never able to live up to her potential, according to Gerry. Which meant, I guess, she never "threw multiples."

The Chicken or the Egg?

After Gerry had transformed our hillside into sheep pasture, the plateau below our bay window into a goat pen, and our detached garage into a rabbit-breeding warren, he made the executive decision to expand into poultry because Pete gave him 30 fertilized eggs and loaned him an incubator. Gerry set this contraption up in the spare bedroom. Thus began three weeks of watching, waiting, and turning eggs every eight hours. Using a permanent marker, he made a black X on one side of every egg. X's up. X's down. Day after day.

On Day 20, hatching commenced with hairline cracks and hollow-sounding cheeps. Within a few hours, 29 slimy chicks sprawled amid the chaos of cracked shells. Only one egg remained whole. Even though he had read that he was to leave the chicks in the incubator for two days, Gerry fretted. They looked so wet and feeble and they thrashed about amid the chaos of eggshells and emerging siblings. Worried that they might catch a chill or cut their little wings on those sharp edges, or crush one another because of overcrowding, he decided to help them out a bit. He moved the chicks to a large cardboard box and rigged a heat lamp inches overhead. Then he tossed all the broken shells in the garbage, leaving the lone unhatched egg in the incubator. We went to bed, and Gerry was grinning as he was lulled to sleep by a cacophony of peeping. I put a pillow over my head and dreamed of wolves dressed like sheep.

Silence Isn't Always Golden

Around four o'clock Gerry shook me awake and asked, "Do you hear anything?"

I listened. Blessed silence. I rolled over.

"There's no chirping!" he yelled as he leaped out of bed and dashed away to check. He returned moments later and slumped onto the bed. "They're all dead. Every one. Their tiny tongues are hanging out." He was devastated.

A few hours later, the thirtieth egg—a late bloomer—hatched. Gerry left that chick in the incubator for two days—no heat lamp this time. That chick grew and flourished and eventually had the run of the property. She laid eggs like land mines all over the garden and yard. She made messes on our front step that I had to dodge, but Gerry let her be because, as the sole survivor of the heat wave, she deserved to live, he said.

The following winter, the first of the nine pregnant rabbit does Gerry purchased began to line her birthing box with fur. Gerry had read in his most recent library loaner, *Raising Rabbits the Modern Way*, that three days before giving birth the doe will use her teeth to pull out fur from the dewlap under her chin and use it to line her nest.

But it was winter, and our garage, one end of which was filled with rabbit cages, wasn't heated. Gerry worried that those naked little babies would freeze so...yep, out came the trusty heat lamp. He rigged the lamp inches above the nest box shortly after the mother had given birth to eight tiny, pink, wiggly little bunnies. When he went back to check on them hours later they weren't wiggling anymore. They were warm though—so warm they died of heat exhaustion.

"You'd think the chicken fiasco would have taught me a lesson,"

Gerry moaned. "But no, I still didn't get it until I did the same thing to some baby bunnies."

A Lesson Learned

"At that point," Gerry says, " I got it. The lesson I learned? Don't try to improve on God's simple plan." God's plan for nature mirrors His plan for humanity: leave the complicated stuff to Him and keep it simple. What I mean is that the creation of life and the miracle of reproduction—God's work—is highly complex. So complex that mankind can't replicate it. By comparison, our job is relatively simple. In the case of the rabbit doe, her God-given instinct guided her to build a nest with her excess fur just in time for the babies to be born. In our case, as followers of Christ, if we are pursuing the dreams God has given us, He will give us the clarity we need when we need it so that we can take the next step. We keep it simple by waiting for clarity, saying yes, and stepping out.

Too often we complicate things by jumping in, like Gerry did with the heat lamp. During my season of waiting for clarity so I could take the next step to pursue my dream as a writer, more than once I wasted time and money trying to turn up the heat and make things happen. Well, things did happen. There was a body count! We turn up the heat when we run ahead of God instead of waiting for Him to make the next step clear. When we complicate God's simple plan, we are in danger of hampering or even killing a perfectly good dream.

Getting Ahead of Yourself

Following God one yes at a time is a simple-life concept. We tend to complicate it when we aren't satisfied with knowing only the next step. We want the whole caboodle up front. Without a detailed itinerary, some of us even refuse to get off the rock. In their book *Simple Life*, authors Thom and Art Rainer put forth four concepts people need in order to move from a complex life to a simple life: clarity, movement, alignment, and focus.[4]

Clarity means knowing where you are going. *Movement*, obviously, is the forward momentum needed to get there. *Alignment* involves figuring out where your life is out of line and making the changes needed to bring it into harmony. And *focus*, usually the toughest task, requires the elimination of good and bad things from our lives.

Four Simple-life Concepts

Let me illustrate the Rainers' four simple-life concepts with an example from my family. Toward the end of our son's third year in school, I grew concerned because he still couldn't read. I hadn't been anxious sooner because JP's French-immersion teachers had assured me that some kids take a little longer to master reading because they are also learning a second language. By this time I knew there must be another problem. I didn't know what it was or what to do, so I called out to God in prayer and asked for clarity. The summer passed in a flurry of activity and before we knew it, school was a week from starting. I still hadn't come up with a solution. JP was scheduled to begin fourth grade French immersion.

Three days before the first day of public school, I interviewed a local community volunteer for a newspaper column I wrote each week. As the interview progressed, I learned that he had once been a public schoolteacher. After 13 years, he and his wife decided to take their kids out of school for a year and travel the world. Since he was already a teacher, he planned to teach his kids, integrating their travels into their lessons. When they returned home, everyone would go back to school, including him. However, by the time they returned, he had decided he would never go back—and neither would his children. He educated all of them at home until they graduated.

Simple

I was intrigued by his story and I asked him if we could talk further off the record. He listened while I poured out my fears and concerns about JP's not being able to read. His first words, gently offered, hit the nail on the head: "I think you already know what to do—you're just scared to do it." He was right. I knew in my heart JP needed one-on-one teaching, and who better to do it than me? Although I'd prayed and asked God to guide me, my fear regarding JP's future combined with my lack of confidence of becoming a home educator kept me glued to the rock.

The barriers that hindered me from following God to pursue the dream He'd planted in my heart to educate my son at home became obvious to me the instant I had *clarity*. Now I had the courage to say yes and get off the rock. Even though I knew the process would be difficult at times, now that I clearly saw the dream, saying yes was a simple thing.

God wants us to know His will, and He will find creative ways to plant His dreams in our hearts. In this case, He spoke clearly to me through the words of a man I was interviewing as part of my secular job. Clarity encouraged *movement*. I took the first step toward the dream and took JP out of school.

And that's when fear kicked in big time, trying to hold me back from pursuing this dream. I was trained to teach literature and essay writing to 16-year-olds who had long ago learned to read. I wasn't trained to teach a can't-sit-still dyslexic 9-year-old how to decipher complex symbols that he said "wouldn't stay still on the page." And what about science, math, physical education, social studies, and health? I wasn't sure where to begin so I again turned to God.

"What about the guy who got you into this mess in the first place?" He said. Well, maybe He said it in a more godly way, but that was the way it translated in my head. I called the community volunteer, burst into tears, got control, and explained my problem. I then took notes while he outlined the steps I needed to take to move forward.

As things progressed that year, I quickly understood I needed to bring my thinking and behavior into *alignment* with my new reality. The desks-in-rows, nine-to-three, teacher-does-the-talking methodology that worked in the classroom had to become something more fluid, interactive, and hands-on. JP learned to read by sitting beside me on the couch for short periods interspersed by long breaks involving physical activity.

When I took JP out of public school, I already had a full schedule so something had to give. In order to *focus* on the homeschooling dream I gave up my afternoon walks, talks, and prayer times with three close friends. Walking was a good thing. Praying with friends was a good thing too. But often it is some of the good things we have to cut out or postpone to pursue our dream and keep life simple.

I didn't read the Rainers' book until ten years after completing my season of homeschooling with JP. If someone had asked me back then to outline the four simple steps I took to achieving my homeschooling dream I wouldn't have said "clarity, movement, alignment, and focus," even though that is precisely what I did. And that's primarily because I don't think in concepts. I think in stories, so I probably would have told you my story and asked you to sift through and find your own catchy terms. Thanks, Thom and Art, for making the process clear.

Trust God to Lead

As delighted as I am to read great books like *Simple Life* and recommend the excellent teaching therein, I know by experience that even if you can't outline what you're doing in four easy steps, if you're following God one yes at a time He will lead you. That's what He did with me. Without knowing the Rainers' four-step process, I lived them out:

- God gave me *clarity:* homeschool my son.

- He prompted me to *get moving* by reminding me of an expert to call.

- One of this man's suggestions was to join a local association of home educators. I went to the first meeting and sat and cried until someone took pity on me (well, okay, I'm just kidding about the tears, but not by much!) and reached out to help. The modeling, advice, and encouragement of these home educators helped bring my thinking and behavior into *alignment.* (And that was a great thing! Our one year of homeschooling turned into five years.)

- And because I was already committed to simpler living, I knew how to *focus* by saying no to even good things in order to realize my dream.

When I first realized that our son needed more than a little extra help after school, my fear for his long-term future and the complexity of deciding which of the various options were best kept me pinned to the rock all summer long. I was waiting for a complete map, detailed itinerary, and an "if I do this it will result in that" verifiable, scientific sureness. But real life seldom provides that. Once I clearly understood what God's dream for my son and me was, and even though I didn't know how it was going to work out, I was able to say yes to following His lead. Simplicity comes with clarity. I stepped off the rock trusting in God's promise that together we would work His plan.

Abraham Gets Off the Rock

Do you remember reading about God telling Abraham to "go out from your land, your relatives, and your father's house to the land that I will show you"?[5] God didn't tell Abraham where to go. All Abraham had was a picture-promise of the dream. He would have to follow God one yes at a time to work the plan. God gave Abraham just enough pieces of the puzzle to get a peek at what it might look like once it was completed. Abraham's primary roles were to believe—to have faith—and to follow. And he climbed off the rock and turned west toward Canaan, the land he had been heading to many years earlier with his father, Terah, who had decided en route to stop and settle in Haran instead (Genesis 11:31). To Canaan and beyond Abraham followed God for approximately 100 years and more than 1200 miles. Abraham died, old and contented, not far from the southern tip of the Dead Sea.[6]

As Abraham journeyed with God, he was given more pieces of the promise puzzle. God told him that He would make him into a great nation, bless him, make his name great, and make him a blessing to all the peoples on the earth.[7] And the way God was going to make Abraham's name great was through his offspring. Now this was even more puzzling to Abraham since he and his wife, Sarah, had no kids—and Sarah was way beyond child-bearing age. Several years passed and no babies come along. Sarah decided God needed a little help so she got out the trusty heat lamp, figuratively speaking, of course.

Sarah suggested Abraham should father a son through her servant Hagar. Abraham complied, and a son was born. They named him

Ishmael, and at last Abraham had an heir. But 13 years later God visits Abraham again and reiterates that he will be the father of nations—but adds that it won't be through Ishmael. No, Abraham's heir will be a son borne by Sarah! Finally Abraham responds like I probably would: He falls to the ground and laughs. "Can a child be born to a hundred-year-old man? Can Sarah, a ninety-year-old woman, give birth?"[8] One year later Sarah delivers Isaac! And even though the promised heir has now arrived, life for mankind will be forever complicated by Abraham and Sarah's attempt to turn up the heat by his fathering Ishmael. Even today Arabs and Israelis are fighting over the real estate Abraham surveyed on his overland trek.

Rather than get bogged down by the complication of Ishmael, let's focus on the *simplicity* of Abraham's relationship with God. When God called him to get up and go, God didn't give him anything more than a dream: Go to a land I will show you. And Abraham wasn't supposed to settle there. No, he was to only pass through and see the scope of the land that would one day be given to his descendants.

At the point of being given the dream, Abraham didn't know how far he would have to go, the route to take, or where the journey would end. Neither did he know how he was going to produce the descendants that would one day inherit the land God was promising. Abraham and Sarah were both well past the parenting stage of life. Talk about impossible! Yet Abraham believed and said yes: "By faith Abraham, when he was called, obeyed and went out to a place he was going to receive as an inheritance; he went out, not knowing where he was going."[9]

All You Really Need to Know

Abraham made some major boo-boos along the way, just like we all do, but God didn't forsake him. He was faithful and was with Abraham to the end. Following God is much simpler when we wait for *Him* to bring us clarity *before* we take the next step. We complicate following God in two ways: 1) getting stuck on the rock, and 2) refusing to move until we have all the details or, conversely, turning up the heat and adding details of our own to speed things up. If we want to follow God and keep it simple, we need to say yes to the dream, step off the rock, and then wait on Him to clearly reveal the next step before we go any further.

When I fly somewhere to speak, many times I'm going someplace I've never been before. Most of the time I've never even met the people who will be picking me up at the airport. Even when I arrive very late a night, if I don't see someone waving me down or holding a sign with my name on it, I don't worry because I know the people who paid to get me there have a vested interest in making sure I arrive. Someone *will* eventually show up. All I have to do is wait. Simple.

When God told Moses to "lead My people, the Israelites, out of Egypt," Moses was nowhere near Egypt.[10] He had left there 40 years earlier on the run from the Pharaoh after murdering an Egyptian.[11] By this time Moses was no longer an impetuous young man easily inflamed by moral ideals. He was a family man, a farmer, a member of the community. He had responsibilities. He was like us—anchored by a mortgage, school fees, credit-card debt, aging parents, college tuitions, car loans, and more. In order to do what God asked, Moses had a lot more "stuff" to pack and things to leave behind than when he had arrived in Midian decades before. That's why I wasn't surprised when Moses reacts to God's call the way I sometimes do, essentially saying, "I'm not moving off this rock until You give me more details!"

An Ordinary Man

Moses' first question to God is, "Who am I that I should go to Pharaoh and that I should bring the Israelites out of Egypt?"[12] Oh, I just love that. Moses must be my long-lost twin. He struggles with the same things I do: lack of confidence, low self-esteem, crippling comparison syndrome. Moses is saying what you and I often say when God gives us "impossible" dreams: "Surely there are others more qualified than me to do this. Go ask them." But God tells Moses the same thing He tells us millennia later: "I will certainly be with you."[13] Remember, God's promise is to take us (go with us), not just send us, as we follow Him to pursue the dreams He gives us. God is assuring Moses that he won't be alone. God will go with him every step of the way.

Just like Abraham, Moses has the promise (the dream), but initially he's too scared to say yes and follow the plan. All he can see are problems. Moses continues to pepper God about all the difficulties: he doesn't know what to say to make the Israelites follow him or to make Pharaoh listen to him. And he doesn't think he's a very convincing speaker, so God should send someone else.[14] By this time, God is fed up so He agrees to allow a team approach. Moses and his brother, Aaron, will go. God promises to help them both by telling them what to say and what to do.

Moses finally gets it. He says yes with his feet by going to his father-in-law and asking permission to return to Egypt. Moses' first yes for this dream. Then he waits. When God reveals to him that those who wanted to kill him are now dead, Moses understands it is time to go. He gathers his wife and sons and the staff God gave him and sets out. That's another yes. Moses and Aaron and company (nobody traveled light in those days) arrive in Egypt, visit Pharaoh, and "drop the bomb." Nine plagues later Pharaoh is finally ready to let his free labor go.

And then God drops another bomb. He tells Moses that He's going to harden Pharaoh's heart so he won't let the people go until his firstborn son is sacrificed. I believe it took a lot of yeses to keep Moses pursuing the dream when Pharaoh continued to deny his request over and over. Even though saying yes usually moves us forward, sometimes we "move forward" by standing our ground and refusing to quit. The adventure that consumed the rest of Moses' life on earth began in earnest once Pharaoh relented and the Israelites followed Moses to their new home just over yonder.

Step by step, yes by yes, God led Moses back to Egypt to gather the people, to convince Pharaoh, to lead the Israelites out of Egypt, and, because of the people's rebellion, to shepherd them for 40 years in the wilderness. God had Moses give them the Law, the foundation for Judaism and, eventually, Christianity.

What makes an impossible dream possible is that *God* simplifies the process by coming along with us and giving us clarity one yes at a time. He really is a lamp for our feet, giving us only enough light for the next step.[15] If I can wait to be picked up with quiet confidence in faraway airports because I trust people I don't even know to care about my welfare, surely I can wait on God, who knows me and loves me, to clearly reveal the next step I am to take.

Dash and Dive

My husband enjoys watching war films, and I occasionally join him. During the gory parts I cover my eyes and ask him to tell me when it's safe to watch again. A typical scene in war films is when the heroes want to take the high ground where the enemy is dug in. Their method usually involves a group of soldiers, one of whom is in charge, who dash from rock to tree to hummock until they get close enough to the enemy that they can toss in grenades or fight hand-to-hand and overcome them, capture them, or force a retreat. The assignment is dangerous, but the method is simple: follow the team leader, dash and dive from cover to cover, and don't stop until you reach the objective. What is drilled into them more than anything else is to obey orders exactly as given. Even if they don't agree with the orders and don't like the officer in command, every soldier is trained to instantly obey.

Follow the Leader

We realize our dreams the same way soldiers reach their military objective: stay focused on the goal but get there in increments, listen for orders, and move out. What makes us freeze up, too scared to make the next dash, is that instead of focusing on the short distance needed for the next segment, we look ahead to the distance between where we are and where the destination is. We panic and don't think we can make it that far. Or maybe the bullets whizzing overhead terrify us so much that we can't move our feet. Or perhaps we lose trust in the Leader and don't think He knows the best route. Or we might fall behind and, once separated from the group, are too scared to forge on alone. Meanwhile, God, our spiritual platoon leader, whispers: "Just run to that tree with Me," and points to a tree we can clearly see just a few feet ahead. "Once we get there, I'll let you know where to run next." Dash by dash, yes by yes, following Him is simple as long as we wait for His clear instructions before making the next dash.

The military metaphor brings up an important point: Advancing into enemy territory is always dangerous. When I say following God is *simple,* I'm not saying it is easy. Often it's not. Sometimes it's so hard that if we had known everything at the beginning, we wouldn't have taken the first step.

God almost always takes us straight into enemy territory. Why? Because He wants to help us defeat the enemies of fear and doubt and anything else that has become a barrier to us experiencing complete freedom in Christ. Freedom has always been worth fighting for. So don't be surprised when you encounter adversity after saying yes to God and doing what He says. But also don't be tempted to complicate the process by taking matters into your own hands or letting yourself freeze up. Actively listen and wait for clear instructions. When you get clarity, say yes. Move forward as far as you can clearly see. When things get murky, stop. Actively listen. Wait for clarity. Say yes. Advance. Stop. Listen. Wait. Simple.

3

IMMEDIATE

*Immediately He made the disciples get into the boat
and go ahead of Him to the other side.*

MATTHEW 14:22

Basma was born into an immigrant Middle-Eastern Muslim family and culture in the United States, but her family moved to Canada during her youth. As a young, unmarried adult woman, she continues to live at home, as is the Arabic custom. Basma has always had a hunger for God. As a Muslim, she was committed to the practices of her faith. Devout Muslims answer the call to prayer five times each day. "I prayed much more than five times a day," she says. "I prayed in the shower, while walking, while driving, while eating. I prayed all the time." But in spite of unceasing prayer, she had no peace. In fact, she now realizes the reason she prayed so much was because she didn't think she would ever be good enough for Allah. She was afraid of her god.

Friendship with Christians in high school opened up an opportunity for her to hear about Jesus. At first she wasn't interested. Her own religion was integral to her family and culture, and she didn't want to rock the family boat. Besides, she had been cautioned by her parents to watch out for the "three-gods-in-one nonsense" of Western culture. Allah was the one true god. They told her that the only reason people "became Christians" was so they could live an unsupervised, sex-crazed, lascivious lifestyle. Her parents believed the historical Jesus was a good teacher but certainly not divine. Basma's main Christian friend continued to live out her faith and talk about her relationship with Jesus. It sounded like Jesus was alive and involved in her life on a personal level, Basma thought. She was intrigued but not convinced. Months later she was in a bookstore with both parents, hurriedly looking for something good to read. Planning to buy the latest teen thriller, she was surprised to find herself holding a copy of *The Prayer of Jabez for Teens*. She didn't know what made her pick up that book. What was even more surprising was that her Muslim dad bought it for her even after seeing the title.

Basma Meets Jesus

While reading her new book later that night, Basma discovered how Jesus could be her friend, her helper, her peace, her Savior. Seventeen years old, midway through Grade 11, all alone in her bedroom in the midst of a family devoted to Islam, Basma gave her heart to Jesus. And He began to change her slowly, in tiny increments. In Grade 12, she met more Christians, and they invited her to attend summer church camp. She was sure her parents wouldn't allow her to go. Basma was shocked when her father said yes. At camp she learned more about Jesus as a personal God, and she began to be cautiously open about her faith.

Today Basma is still careful about how much she shares her new faith with her immediate family. Her mother and sisters-in-law know she is a Christian, but her brothers and father do not. In Middle East culture, family members have been severely punished and even killed for much lesser offenses. Her rejection of Islam puts her in a tenuous and dangerous position. Being found out by the males in her family could result in being forced into a quick move from Canada to the Middle East, where her father could arrange a marriage to a Muslim man of his choice. Basma attends church fairly regularly when she can finagle it. She meets other believers for Bible study, prayer, and fellowship on the university campus where she goes to school. Life at home has not been easy, and Basma often feels alone as she follows God in the midst of difficult circumstances.

Not long ago, Basma began spending a lot of time with a young Muslim man who shared her culture and Arabic language, but not her

Christian faith. In so many ways he was exactly the kind of guy she'd always dreamed of marrying: handsome and articulate, caring and cultured, respectful and kind. Their meetings were kept secret because their families had not met or sanctioned their relationship. Even though they were not officially dating, Basma knew her heart was in deeper than her head. She hadn't told him she was a Christian so her soul was troubled. She worried that if she revealed this potentially explosive information it would bring the relationship to a screeching halt. When her heart became more entangled, she came to me for counsel.

A Difficult Choice

I was instantly concerned about this mixed-faith relationship, knowing it would lead to a very complicated future. We set up a lunch date, and I introduced her to a mother and daughter who were recent converts from Islam. Our time flew by in a flurry of conversation about shared cultural experiences and spiritual encounters. Before we parted, I asked Basma what her prayer needs were. She revealed she had fallen in love with the man she was seeing. I advised her to tell him the truth for the sake of her integrity, if nothing else. I prayed with her that she would have a clear understanding of God's will and know what to do. The other mom at the table soundly reinforced my advice. She explained what it was like to be in a mixed-faith marriage. Only by God's grace was the relationship with her husband surviving at all, she said. It was complicated, difficult, and divisive. "Before you get in any deeper," she advised, "you must tell your young man the truth."

Basma left the luncheon deeply troubled. Praying as she drove, she asked God to clearly reveal His will. It was one of those "let this cup pass from me, but not my will but Yours" prayers. Turning into her neighborhood, she noticed a pizza box on the side of the road. Knowing the pizza company inscribed pithy sayings on the inside covers of their boxes, she felt compelled to retrieve it. She pulled over, jumped out, grabbed the box, and, once inside the car, opened it. She read:

> Words are powerful and can affect more than just the
> ones around you. They are very influential and can be

inspirational or hurtful. It's important to always keep your integrity and speak the truth.

Basma knew this was God's message for her. She had clarity. She knew He wanted her to tell the truth even at the risk of losing her romantic relationship. She said yes by immediately setting up a meeting. When she and her gentleman friend got together, Basma revealed her faith to her friend. It was the beginning of the end. He asked her a lot of questions about Jesus that she couldn't answer. Soon he began to withdraw, and before long he was out of her life completely.

Basma shed many tears, but she says she knows telling him was the right thing to do. And the experience revealed her need for more Bible study, so she's seizing opportunities to delve more deeply into God's truths. She still hopes to marry a man who shares her language and culture, since to do otherwise would mean rejection by her family, but she is willing to trust God to lead her, one yes at a time, to the right man. Even if she has to "settle for a Westerner," she says with a grin.

God wants us to follow Him. Sometimes He uses creative means to get His directives into our hands. When He does and we see the immediate step to take, saying yes is the best response.

Is This Dream from God?

In case confusion has crept in, let's clarify what we've covered so far because it's best to thoroughly understand before diving into deeper waters.

If you have asked God to forgive your sin (of living without Him, of being your own god, of running your own life) and your sins (activities and thoughts that didn't line up with God's principles and truths), and asked Him to be Lord of your life, then you have accepted His free gift of forgiveness and eternal life He purchased for you on the cross. You are a child of God—a Christian, a believer.

Becoming a Christ-follower is the first step. Now you get to discover *how to follow Christ* on a day-to-day basis. If that's where you are, this book is perfect for you. God has an *overarching purpose* for your life as a Christian. Everything He leads you to do or to become feeds into that main purpose, which is to make you more like Christ so you can be His hands and feet on earth. (And if you've been a Christian for quite a while, this book will help you more quickly identify and follow God's dreams for you.)

Under the umbrella of *purpose*, God gives us many *overlapping dreams* or *picture-promises*. If you're not sure if the dream you are seeing is a picture-promise from God, ask these simple questions:

- Will realizing this dream make me more like Christ?
- Will pursuing this dream allow me to be His hands and feet on earth?
- Will this dream have a positive impact on the world or does it further my own interests and ambitions?
- Is this dream consistent with what the Bible teaches?
- Has this dream been affirmed through wise Christian counsel?

Once you have satisfactorily determined the dream is from God, you are ready to say yes with your feet. At this point, you are sitting on your meditation rock where God has spoken clearly to you. You are either clinging to the rock in fear and uncertainty or you are actively listening for Him to clearly reveal the next move. Or have you already leaped off the rock and are running ahead of Him with your heat lamp in hand?

Following God Turn by Turn

By now if you don't already own a GPS (Global Positioning System) you have certainly heard of them, seen them, or had access to one. The basics of how GPS works is that the driver inputs his or her destination and the GPS guides the driver, turn by turn, to that destination. When the device is initially activated and the driver is parked off a roadway, the GPS advises the driver to "proceed to the highlighted route" so that it can begin giving directions. After getting on the highlighted route, the driver follows the road he is on until alerted by the GPS to turn.

The most obvious difference between a GPS and a paper map is that the driver doesn't have to see the entire route, choose the best roadways, and be on constant alert for signs indicating where to turn. He simply has to follow the last directive until a new directive is given. And the real beauty to a GPS is the "recalculating" feature. If the GPS gives a directive and the driver hesitates, questioning whether it's the right way to go, he may overshoot the turn. The GPS then declares in a rather disgusted tone, "Recalculating." Then the machine provides a new set of directions that takes the driver from the point he's at to the destination. It provides an alternate route or tells the driver to "please make a legal U-turn" and go back to do what was directed in the first place.

Without stretching this illustration to the breaking point, I think this is a good picture of us. We're parked atop our meditation rocks waiting for a dream and clarity before taking the first step. Sometimes the first step is nothing more than an area God illuminates, and we need to move in that direction to hear His next directive. Like using a GPS, we follow God one directive at a time. Some of these directions are like "continue 83 miles on highway 279," but most of them are "drive one-half mile and turn left on Brentwood Doctor Northwest" (for some weird reason my GPS thinks "Dr." means "doctor," not "Drive").

Difficult Directives

When we follow God, occasionally He gives us a directive that doesn't seem to lead to our destination. This is surely what Abraham must have thought when God told him to sacrifice his son Isaac. He must have wondered how killing his only son would lead to the dream God had given him of being the father of nations. I've had similar experiences—not being asked to sacrifice a child but wondering if I heard God correctly. "God, did I hear You right? You want me to do what?"

I've mentioned that God gave me the dream to be a writer when I was in my twenties. So you can probably imagine how excited I was when I finally had a book proposal accepted and was offered a contract by a publishing house shortly after my fortieth birthday. But as I followed God "turn by turn," He made it clear that I was not to sign the contract. There was no ram in the thicket as there had been for

Abraham to replace Isaac on the altar.[1] My book died before it was ever born. Months of work went up in smoke.

Even though I was downhearted and discouraged, wondering if I would ever reach the destination and realize God's dream for me, I continued to follow His directives, albeit with plodding feet. God knew best, of course. He could see around blind corners where I couldn't. He knew that just a few "turns" ahead I would embark on a home-schooling journey with our son that would require much of my attention. Another book proposal, another contract, another publishing house, and the publication of my first book were all part of the plan, but it was further down the road than I had thought (and hoped!) it would be.

Did I Hear That Right?

How do you respond when God reveals the next turn He wants you to take? If you're like me, you sometimes doubt, question, weigh the options, or ask Him to repeat the directions because you hope you heard Him wrong. You might hesitate, allowing fear to hold you back. Occasionally you might stall for time, hoping He'll send a different turn that will take you down a street you think is better. Sometimes we have a hard time understanding His directions (discerning God's will), which can result in confusion and inertia.

Even though evangelical Christians are fond of saying "God told me to…" very few of us ever hear audible directions. And I know of no one who has seen writing on the wall (see Daniel 5). However, as Basma's story illustrates, God is not limited in any way when it comes to getting His directives to us in the nick of time. He almost always uses trusted methods, such as Bible-based teaching, preaching, personal Bible study, godly counsel, and the urging of the Holy Spirit. But every now and then, when we really need it, God colors outside those lines and plants a pizza box in our path.

Before you go skidding off track with this bit of information, let me assure you that if you think you are receiving a directive from God via an unconventional medium and it goes against biblical truth and godly advice, disregard it! When Dr. Frankie Rainey, one of my Bible college professors, was a pastor, a man came to his church office one afternoon seeking counsel. He told Pastor Rainey that "God told him" to leave his wife and three small children and marry his secretary, whom he loved. "I'm so confused! What should I do?" he asked.

"I have some very good news for you!" Pastor Rainey exclaimed. "That message wasn't from God!" Dr. Rainey's confidence about the source of the message was founded on sound biblical doctrine: God hates divorce. He instituted the sacrament of marriage, and God considers marriage vows lifelong promises of faithfulness. Sadly, the man wasn't really seeking counsel. He wanted pastoral blessing on what he'd planned to do anyway. Had he been seeking counsel, he would have followed it, but he did not and two families and many hearts were shattered as a result.

The Strong-willed Child

When Gerry and I had our first baby, we thought she was a perfect little doll. We were so smitten that we had a hard time disciplining her when she began to assert her will. Everything she did was so precious! As a result, by the time Christine was two we had created a monster—"Frankenstine." We couldn't leave her with anyone or take her anywhere without her ruining the experience with her unruly behavior. We were vaguely aware that her bad behavior was a parenting problem, but we were so entrenched in our bad habits that we didn't have a clue how to turn things around.

One Sunday afternoon while chatting outside after church with a friend and mentor who was also a pastor's wife, God spoke clearly to me through her words. When I expressed my fear for the future regarding my strong-willed child, who was already an unmanageable toddler, she said, "I found that if you get control of a child when she's small, you won't have to worry about her when she is a teen." This woman who had raised seven wonderful kids was used by God to tell me important information: Get this child under control before it is too late! So simple, so profound, but not all that easy to do. The key was to start now.

Gerry and I prayed, asking God to show us the first step. We actively listened for God and earnestly sought solutions. Within days we discovered that a brand-new Bible study in a nearby church was about to begin using material from Dr. James Dobson. We signed up! As we watched the *Strong-Willed Child* video series, read the book, and put the principles into action, we saw remarkable changes in the behavior of our toddler. It wasn't without a lot of tears from parents and child and the desire to go back to our old carefree ways, but God encouraged us with small victories as we followed Him one yes at a time. Today that difficult toddler is a wonderful mother who is successfully raising her own strong-willed kids.

Reaching the Destination

Peter and his fellow disciples learned that while *immediate* obedience doesn't guarantee smooth sailing, it does promise the assurance of reaching the other side. When Jesus finished feeding 5000 people with two fish and five loaves on a hillside overlooking Lake Galilee, He gave the disciples a simple, *immediate* directive: get in the boat and row to the other side. This story, in Matthew 14, tells about the terrifying storm that the disciples encountered as they were rowing across the lake in the middle of the night. Their immediate obedience took them straight into rough waters! Obedience often comes with adversity. Sometimes it seems like obedience even invites trouble.

If obedience pretty much guarantees trouble, why should we say yes? My answer is that I would much rather be walking hand-in-hand with Jesus across a storm-tossed sea than lying facedown in the desert of spiritual dryness, wondering where God went or if God exists. Certainty, even accompanied by struggle, is far more attractive than doubt accompanied by dead stillness. Forward momentum is preferable to inertia.

So what's the key to success? When you follow God one yes at a time, you only need to concern yourself with His last directive. What was the last thing He told you to do? Are you doing it? If so, keep going on the road you're on until you hear Him tell you to turn. And don't forget to take time to enjoy the scenery!

As long as you are actively listening and earnestly seeking, God will clearly reveal the next turn you must take. Like Peter on the sea, each step toward Jesus is another yes. When Peter took his eyes off Jesus and looked down at the waves, he began to sink because his focus had shifted to the impossible—walking on water. It's the same with us. Keeping our eyes on God, we say yes by immediately obeying His directive, and then the next, and the next, and the next until we realize the dream He's given us. Because we have Jesus "in our boat," we will always get to the other side.

Say Yes Now

Immediate obedience means we say yes *now*. Even though we don't always know how we'll achieve the goal, we say yes. Our yes means we step out even though it looks like we're stepping into the unknown. *Immediate* also refers to *time*. God often gives us long-term dreams but short-term directives. When listening for His guidance, understand that it will involve your immediate future—hours, days, weeks, months, or years. God directs us to take the next turn. We need to only worry about taking the next step. When we're following God one yes at a time, we're letting Him lead turn-by-turn until we reach the destination. God says, "Take *this* turn now, and let me handle how we're getting to our destination."

Immediate also refers to *position*, as in "kick the ball that is immediately in front of us." What is right in front of us must be dealt with before we can deal with the next thing. There will be cases where God has clearly spoken to you, making it *simple* enough so you know exactly what He wants you to do. For example, "Speak to your coworker about your relationship with God." However, office logistics, time constraints, family commitments, and so forth may mean the conversation does not occur for several weeks. In cases like that, *immediate* means "the next thing you do as soon as you are able to do it."

Stranded on the Summit

I recently came across a newspaper story about Denis Shakel's challenge to survive. He was stranded alone on the summit of a mountain in New Zealand wearing only shorts and a light shirt. During the night the temperature plunged to minus 22 degrees Fahrenheit.[2] Earlier that day, Denis had set out on a short trek with his brother-in-law. Expecting to make it to the summit and back again during daylight hours, they didn't take along warm clothing or any type of shelter. A tragic accident killed his hiking companion near the top of the mountain, which delayed Shakel's descent until nightfall, by which time it was too dangerous to try to find his way down in the dark. How was he going to make it through a wintery night wearing only summer clothing?

The only way he made it, he says, was by setting his goal (the dream) on seeing the sun come up and then breaking down the grueling eight hours ahead into five-second increments. When the sun went down he began to count, one icy breath after another up to five. Then he started over again. Thousands of times, he repeated his five-second count until he made it through "the longest night of my entire life."[3] By reducing this impossible dream (survive the night) into something *simple* (count to five) and *immediate,* it became *possible.* Shakel survived. Five seconds at a time he stayed awake. Five seconds at a time he fought the drowsiness that is the subtle killer for people with hypothermia. Every five seconds he congratulated himself on making his goal, and then he started again, focusing on getting through the next five seconds.

One Day at a Time

That long, cold, life-threatening night, Shakel practiced the same principle that has given hope and success to recovering alcoholics all over the world who found sobriety and serenity by learning to live one day at a time. The founders of AA, desperate addicts themselves, knew that making big promises to quit drinking had never worked for them; whereas breaking down the goal into bite-size chunks of time was one of the keys to unlocking the mystery of addiction recovery. In the first days of recovery, alcoholics literally manage minute to minute. Each hour is a victory. Each day, a mountain climbed. Every day begins with the hope that, just for today, they will choose sanity instead of sickness. And one day at a time, new lives are built.

Shakel is a professor who teaches management at the University of Western Ontario's Richard Ivey School of Business. He has incorporated into his teaching the profound lesson he learned that night: "the importance of approaching seemingly insurmountable challenges by stepping back and breaking them into smaller, more manageable pieces, all the while keeping your eye on the long-term goal."[4]

Following God one yes at a time provides a way for Christians (and anyone else, for that matter) who have made big promises in the past and failed to live up to them, to finally taste success one *simple, immediate, possible* yes at a time. That's how people write books. It is how championships are won, nations are formed, marriages succeed, cancer is conquered, summits are scaled, and God-sized dreams are realized.

What Was the Last Thing He Said?

When God clearly speaks, your job is to say yes and follow His directive right now. You can do it because you know you can trust Him with your future. He will make sure to get you to the destination. You don't need to worry about all those future twists and turns in the road. Just focus on the last thing He told you to do. If you sense God is pointing you in a certain direction but you aren't sure where to start, look for the *simple, immediate, possible* step that will lead toward your destination (dream). It is simple if you *clearly understand* what to do. It is immediate if it is the *next step* you must take. It is possible if you *can* do it.

Sometimes God gives us dreams to which we already know most of the steps. So instead of guiding us by giving us the steps to take, His role is to encourage us, strengthen us, empower us, and get us back on track when we take a wrong turn. Other times, the dreams He gives involve what we've never tried before. In those cases, His directives include steps that teach us and guide us to acquire the skills, training, and experience we need to ensure we "make it to the other side."

Remember, God's in the boat with us. He's "rowing" with us. He doesn't send us; He *takes* us. So have you said yes to the last directive He gave? If not, say yes immediately!

4

POSSIBLE

The impossible dream God gave Gerry atop that large rock in Saskatchewan was realized five years later in California. What made it possible was that right from the start we heard and obeyed *simple* (clear; not necessarily easy), *immediate* (right in front of us; the next step), *possible* (doable) directives and trusted God to take us to our destination (dream) as we followed Him one yes at a time. Sometimes we had to hold the course, refusing to quit when times got tough. Sometimes we knew there was a turn ahead but weren't sure which way to turn so we had to stop and wait on God to give us clarity. Following God to realize an impossible dream *is* possible when you trust that the One who told you to "get in the boat" will come to you in the midst of the storms and see you through to the other side.[1] Our job, we learned repeatedly, was simply to do what the disciples knew they must do to stay afloat—head into the wind and keep rowing.

When God revealed His dream for Gerry to continue his education, by human standards the timing was wrong. We had two babies that I had left my career to raise in response to my own "rock encounter" where I said yes to God's dream for me to be a stay-at-home mom. And even if I'd had a job, moving to the United States meant I couldn't work because of visa restrictions. (We chose an American seminary because our denomination didn't have one in Canada at that time.) We had no savings and nothing of value to cash in or sell. We were already living on a tight budget, relying heavily on food we grew in our garden and meat we raised on the acreage surrounding the church.

Moving 1200 miles across an international boundary to a place where I couldn't work and the options for Gerry's employment were strictly limited was crazy. However, Gerry and I had the great fortune of having been baptized and mentored by Henry Blackaby, who later cowrote with Claude King the popular book *Experiencing God*. He taught us to recognize a God-sized task as something only God could do. This seminary education dream was obviously a huge undertaking so we simply trusted God to see us through. We got in the boat and started rowing to the other side.

Leaving Shore

Gerry still had one year remaining to complete his undergrad degree, so the first move was from our lakeside pastorate to the city where the Canadian university was located that Gerry was going to enroll in. It was already mid-August when Gerry got his "rowing" orders, which meant we only had two weeks to get resettled before classes began. We found a cockroach-infested house at the right price in the worst part of the city, moved in, cleaned it up, and continued with pastoral ministry in a new church. By stretching every dollar until it screamed for mercy, we fed our family, met our bills, financed Gerry's education, and made it through. One year later, bachelor's degree in Gerry's hand, we packed up and prepared for the bigger move.

With the departure date nearing, we still didn't have the means to make the 1200-mile journey that was supposed to take four days. All we had was the absolute assurance that God had told us to get in the boat and row to the other side. So one-by-one we did *simple, immediate, possible* things and slowly made our way out into open water. We completed the paperwork; sorted, stored and packed our things; planned the itinerary; and trusted that God would make a way.

A few weeks before leaving, a young couple from our church, who were also students and just as poor as we were, knocked on our door after supper one night and handed us the keys to their beloved Datsun pickup. The little Datsun was already long in the tooth, but she looked pretty spiffy from the outside—bright yellow, shiny, and clean. We were astounded at their generosity. They said God had clearly told them to give the truck to us, and they immediately obeyed. We were so grateful! Now we had a way to get our stuff via the Datsun mini-truck, and ourselves via our Mazda hatchback to our destination.

The Mazda was another miracle. We got her from a former church member who specialized in rebuilding cars. To say she was used was an understatement—abused would have been more accurate. Our Mazda started life as two Mazdas. She was rebuilt from the two good halves leftover from a head-on and a rear-ender. She was given to us in trade for our full-sized newer truck whose engine had blown. (That's a story for another time.) The Mazda was neon orange.

The Beverly Hillbillies Sans Granny

Now we had the wheels but we still didn't have the wherewithal. Barring any surprises, we thought we had enough cash to make the trip, but beyond that we had nothing for rent or food or tuition. Trusting God with the *impossible* dream, we did the next *possible* thing. We rented and loaded a small U-Haul trailer. By the time we were done shoehorning everything in, it took two men to shut the back door. We piled everything else in the bed of the Datsun. To create a little more packing space, we flipped four kitchen chairs upside down and wedged their backs just inside the tailgate. The upended chair bottoms stuck out behind the truck like a cantilevered closet on a house. Onto those chair bottoms, I bungeed more goods including my 20-pound bag of whole-wheat flour (my little bit of manna insurance). We were going to need bread when we got there, I thought, and who knew where a person could buy a good loaf of Canadian prairie-grown, stone-ground, whole-wheat bread in America. By the time we were loaded, we looked just like the Clampetts, sans Granny in the rocker, headed for Beverly Hills.

Heading into Deep Water

Before long, moving day arrived and off we went, praying there would be no storms along the way. Gerry led the way to the border in the Datsun with the trailer in tow. I followed in the Mazda with the toddlers and Glenda, our friend and godsend, who came along to help with the children. (She would fly home.) We made it to the border on the afternoon of the second day. Even though he had researched extensively and had all our paperwork in triplicate, Gerry was as jittery as a stowaway when he was invited into the border kiosk for further questioning by the customs agent. And for good reason, one look at our traveling rig hinted that we could be a big drag on the American economy. Moments later Gerry rushed out of the building with a wide-eyed look of incredulity and hurried over to where we were picnicking on the grass.

"We're approved! Let's get out of here!" Gerry blurted. More quietly he added, "Before they take a second look at us and change their minds."

The Wind Begins to Blow

I had food to pack up, diapers to change, and the car to rearrange so by the time I was finally ready, Gerry looked like he would implode. We got in our vehicles and suddenly I realized I didn't have my keys. Glenda didn't have them either. I hollered over to Gerry before he drove away and asked if he had them. He did not. Two hours later, after unpacking the entire back half of the Mazda, we found the keys. They had slipped through a hole in the lining of the diaper bag.

Gerry was not happy—seriously not happy. The time saved at the border because of his hard work was now lost. One look at his face made me question the wisdom of moving to a country where guns are legal. Then I got a great idea. I knew that he had been cloistered in the truck for two days with no radio, no music, no one to talk to. While this would have been heaven for me, it was slow torture for Gerry.

"Why don't we switch vehicles?" I suggested. "Then you can listen to the news and talk to Glenda." I didn't mention the two cranky toddlers who commandeered the radio with demands for their favorite cassettes to be played nonstop. Gerry wasn't sure it was a good idea for me to pull the trailer in a truck with standard transmission. I reminded him of the 100-mile journey I had made in the truck a month earlier, during which the clutch had failed entirely. I had been forced to guess when to shift based on the sound of the rpms. I assured him I could manage. He finally smiled, gave me a hug, and we exchanged keys.

The Sea Gets Choppy

The first few miles were uneventful as I began to get the feel for pulling the overloaded little rig. But as we got into the foothills and then the first mountain, the Datsun went slower and slower. I knew the little truck only had four cylinders, but it felt like three of them had asthma. I limped up the mountain with the eager little Mazda hard on my tail. In my side mirror I watched Gerry pulling out and pulling in, pulling out and pulling in again. He never passed; he just added sideways miles to his cumulative total as an expression of his frustration. Finally he flashed his lights, our signal to pull over and palaver. We convened on the highway shoulder.

"Can't you give it more gas?" he asked in his French-Canadian way that includes enough arm signals to marshal a jet to its dock at the airport.

"Do you want me to pedal with my feet like Fred Flintstone?" I wailed, adding my own rendition of a flight attendant indicating exits fore and aft. He reminded me that we were almost three hours behind schedule now, and he wouldn't be surprised if there wasn't an available hotel room for the next 500 miles.

"I'm doing my best. Stay off my tail! You're making me a nervous wreck," I hollered. Ah, the sweet things we say when the oars begin to chafe. We stomped back to our vehicles and set out once again, chugging up the mountain like the little engine that thought he could. The sun began to set. I grumbled, feeling sorry for myself, but kept the gas pedal mashed to the floor. Top speed was about 30 miles per hour.

Between a Rock and a Deep Place

At long last, with a gasp and a wheeze, we crested the last mountain in this range and began to head down the other side. Gravity was my friend. I shifted into the highest gear, took my foot completely off the gas, and allowed the weight of the trailer to push the little pickup faster and faster. "I'll bet he's happy now!" I exulted as tree branches slapped against the side of the truck when I veered too close to the mountainside, which I did often, fearing the abyss on the other side of the road. Pretty soon I was going so fast I began to feel a little scared of the slapping branches and fishtailing trailer. I tapped the brakes. No response.

Okay, I thought, *maybe this is one of those deals where you have to pump the brakes.* I pumped the brakes and felt little tugs that slowed me ever so slightly. *Okay,* I thought, *maybe this is one of those deals where you have to put both feet on the brakes, lock your knees, and confess all your sins because you're going to see Jesus.* Gripping the wheel like a *Titanic* survivor on a floating plank, I promised God the moon as I hurtled down the mountain under the darkening sky. Unrelenting pressure on the inadequate brakes slowed me just enough to "keep 'er between the ditches," as partygoers like to say at evening's end in my hometown.

Miraculously I made it to level ground alive and intact. The truck shuddered to a halt and died like a buckin' bronco ridden to lathery submission. I hadn't downshifted because I was too frozen with terror to unlock my knees. Peeling my stiff fingers off the steering wheel one by one, I shakily rolled down the window and gulped the cool night air. I looked in the mirror, expecting to see the Mazda right behind me. I had visualized our glorious reunion in my mind. Gerry would run to me, rip open my door, pull me into his arms, cradle me, kiss my tearstained cheeks, thank God with loud cries for sparing my life, promise to take better care of me in the future—all this and more as the background music swelled. Once I had milked it for all it was worth, I would ask Gerry, "Did we test the brakes *before* or *after* we loaded the Datsun and hooked on a fully stuffed trailer?" But there was no car behind me.

Real Life vs. Hollywood

Several minutes passed before the headlights of the Mazda finally came into view. She skidded to a stop right behind me on the gravel shoulder. Gerry leaped out and ran up to my open window. He thrust his head in the open window close enough to kiss me so I squeezed out some tears and puckered up.

"Man!" he bellowed. "Did you make good time coming down that mountain!" He was thoroughly impressed with my driving.

I was speechless. *We* are *the Clampetts,* I thought. *And I got Jethro.* I quickly and not-so-calmly relayed the reasons for my time-saving adventure. With plenty more mountains yet to cross, we knew what we needed to do next before we could continue. We spent the following day and the rest of our money getting the Datsun's brakes replaced in a little town in Idaho. That unforeseen catastrophe could have marked the end of an impossible dream because we had run out of all the money *we* had been able to save for our trip. Just like the disciples, over a mile from land and being battered by the waves because of the wind, we were partway between where we embarked and where we were headed. We were well out into open water and being buffeted to and fro.[2]

When the storm hit, the disciples were terrified. And I was terrified during my roller coaster ride down the mountain. Some of the younger, inexperienced disciples probably wanted to quit rowing and hang on for dear life, fearing they might get washed overboard by the next big wave. But they knew that the minute they let go of the oars they would turn broadside and be swamped. I was "in the same boat" wanting to cover my eyes and scream but knowing I had to hang on to the wheel and keep the truck from catapulting into the chasm on one side or crashing into the mountain wall on the other.

Blinded

When Jesus told His followers to get into the boat and row to the other side, He wasn't surprised when a storm blew in. As a matter of fact, He already knew the storm was on its way. He was planning to go to them, over the storm-tossed sea, and make sure they got to the other side. I believe the reason we often miss seeing God's work in our lives today is because, just like the disciples who initially thought they were seeing a ghost, we are so blinded by our immediate *environment*, our past *experiences,* and our inadequate *expectations* that we don't recognize Jesus.[3] In our case, Jesus came to us even before the storm hit and gave us what we needed to weather it, but it took us a while to recognize Him because our prior experience had conditioned us to expect something else.

The Jesus We Don't Recognize

The night before we discovered the need for brake repair, we had stayed at my brother's house in Southern Alberta. Jim is two years older than me and the only boy in our family. He built a successful business in the boom-and-bust oil industry in Alberta. Jim had privately slipped an envelope into Glenda's hand before we left his house the morning of the wild ride, telling her not to show it to me until we were 100 miles down the road. I guess he didn't want to endure my probably teary-eyed gratitude. I can't blame him, I suppose. He'd been through enough drama growing up with seven sisters to last a lifetime.

We hadn't crossed the border before Glenda, with a squeal, thrust the envelope in my face. "It feels like it's full of money!" she shouted. It was. Jim's generous, totally unexpected gift took us all the way to California, paid our rent, and bought our groceries until Gerry's first earnings took over. The $160 we'd left home with was what it cost, to the penny, to repair the Datsun's brakes.

It's All His

My brother, Jim, isn't a Christ-follower. God's gift to us through Jim, coming from secular rather than sacred sources was an unexpected avenue of blessing that temporarily blinded us to the fact that this was Jesus, walking across the waves, coming to help us in our storm. Once we had the time to reflect, we were awakened to something we hadn't yet grasped about God: He can access the wealth of anyone He pleases and funnel it to whomever He chooses, whenever He chooses:

> We serve a God so powerful He created an entire universe out of nothing. He holds every star and galaxy in its place. He took a lump of clay and created a human being. He gives life to every person on earth. There's *nothing* God cannot do...God has proven throughout history that no human condition or situation exceeds His ability to do a miracle. The limiting factor is always us.[4]

We wouldn't have been caught off-guard by gifts of money from our church family or our Christian friends because they understood and supported and admired our desire to follow God into the unknown. The extremely generous gift of the Datsun came from the hand of other believers, so we were incredibly grateful to our friends and recognized God's hand at work. But the gift from my brother was the "Jesus we didn't expect." Our eyes were opened even wider to God's loving provision and personal care for us. We began to see how impossible dreams become *possible* when God *takes* us to our destination.

Rowing a Little Further

We realize the impossible by saying yes to the *simple, immediate,* and *possible*. Sometimes "possible" means "recalculating." (Remember the GPS metaphor?) It means having to adjust our plans. That's why it took us five years to complete our four-year dream. Gerry needed to take a lighter load of courses when he accepted the role of senior pastor midway through his second year at seminary. He became a long-distance commuter from his pastorate in Modesto to the seminary near San Francisco.

Even though it took a year longer, the love, support, and encouragement of those wonderful people helped us make it to our destination. That church in Modesto was Jesus walking across the waves over and over in the storms we went through. They helped us row by bringing groceries to us when one of our babysitters noticed our cupboards were bare. They loaned us vehicles when ours needed fixing. They invited us for meals. They slipped cash into our pockets. They acted like grandparents to our children and family for Gerry and me. They laughed with us, cried with us, worked with us, and celebrated with us when Gerry received his degree. They even threw a baby shower for me in absentia—photographed the gathering of women and mailed the gifts and well wishes and party favors to me in a box—when I had a baby nine months after we left California.

Jesus Calms Us First

Jesus comes to us in many forms during our storms. Sometimes we recognize Him right away and sometimes it takes us a little longer. Even though we want nothing more than for Him to stop the boat from rocking, the first thing He does is calm us in the midst of the storm.[5] The Scripture doesn't say Jesus helped the disciples row to the other side once He got into the boat. When Jesus stepped onboard, "at once the boat was at the shore where they were heading" (John 6:21). We can infer that it was much easier for the disciples to keep rowing once their fears and the sea were stilled. So even without putting His hand to the oars, Jesus helped get them to the other side. And He continues to work that way in our lives today. His physical hand doesn't pull the oars of our boats, but His calming presence and spiritual power help us keep rowing steadily, stroke by stroke, toward our dreams.

Keep Rowing

The insights Denis Shakel discovered during his long, horrendous night as he conquered high-altitude hypothermia, are told in his book *Five Seconds at a Time: How Leaders Can Make the Impossible Possible.* This book holds merit for everyone, not just leaders. Denis says,

> Too often, people can look at a daunting challenge and get caught in indecision about whether they can overcome it. But there is a profound difference when you start with the assumption that any goal can be achieved, and break down the task of getting there into small pieces. From that point, all you have to do is ask yourself what's the next step and then take it. It's important to keep remembering the ultimate goal and never allow doubt to undermine your confidence.[6]

Shakel had a dream: to stay alive until morning. He didn't know how he could do it; it seemed impossible given the conditions. Instead of allowing the impossible dream to overwhelm and defeat him, he figured out what *was* possible. He knew he could stay alive for the next five seconds. He did something *simple, immediate, possible* and lived to see the sun come up the next morning. Your dream may look impossible, but what is one *simple, immediate, possible* thing you *can* do today to take you one inch closer to the finish line?

The Barriers Are in Our Heads

Rick Hansen is a Canadian wheelchair athlete and humanitarian whose foundation raises millions of dollars for spinal cord injury research. Known as the "Man in Motion," his fame dates back to his 26-month Man in Motion tour that began in Vancouver, British Columbia, in March 1985. He headed out in his wheelchair and logged more than 40,000 km (almost 25,000 miles) through 34 countries on four continents before crossing Canada and ending back in Vancouver in May 1987. He raised more than $26 million for spinal cord research and quality of life initiatives.

When Rick was 15, he and some of his buddies hitched a ride in the back of a truck. His spinal cord was severed when he was thrown from the truck after it collided with a car. The personal philosophy that has seen Rick Hansen through the accomplishment of impossible dreams (his latest is to raise $200 million for spinal cord research in two years), is "Dwell not on what you don't have, or can't have; focus on *what you have* and *are able to do.*"[7] In other words, focus on what is *simple, immediate, possible.* And I would add "trust God to get you to the other side and realize the dream."

Hansen, now 52, is a paralympian gold medalist and was one of the torchbearers for the 2010 Winter Olympics in Vancouver, Canada. In an interview on his latest goal, he said this about reaching for impossible dreams:

> Usually the biggest demon is not out there. It's what's inside your head. That was one of the most profound lessons I've learned in my life. I would never give that up for the use of my legs.[8]

I encourage you to keep working toward your dreams. Don't let doubt erode your confidence. What is impossible for people is possible for God![9]

In our move to California, God proved to Gerry and me that the barriers that keep us from following God—the things that make us want to quit rowing—are almost always internal. What we thought were material barriers, such as no funds, no jobs, two babies, foreign country, turned out to be *mental* barriers that God overcame as we followed Him one oar dip at a time. It may look like the "other side" is a long way off, but you only need to ask, Can I dip the paddle one more time? Your answer will be yes if your dream is from God, you're following Him closely and listening intently for His directions, and you are willing to make course corrections as needed.

5

GOD SPEAKS

The question...is not whether God speaks to his people, but how he does so. [1]

HENRY BLACKABY

By now you're probably intrigued by the idea of pursuing the *dream* God has given to you by following Him one *simple, immediate, possible* yes at a time. I hope you're eager to test this process yourself. However, if you're not in the habit of hearing from God or you're unsure of the sound of His voice, you might be wondering how you can know His dream for you?

How can we discern the voice of God and recognize His activity? How can we see the hand of God at work? In a Bible study that changed the vernacular of Christians all over the world, Henry Blackaby and Claude King instructed believers who wanted to follow God to *look for where God is working and join Him.* [2] I couldn't agree more. (I don't think there is any better Bible study and teaching on the planet than *Experiencing God* for helping believers know and do God's will. I have worked through the study on my own as well as taught this life-changing material to groups. I encourage you to read it!) I learned the hard way that you can't "join" a God you aren't listening for or seeking or are willing to be found by.

My decade in the wilderness of spiritual dryness alerted me to the sad reality that Christians can wander so far from God that they no longer see Him or hear Him or recognize His involvement in their lives or anyone else's. That's what happened to me and countless others I've met and heard from. Is that your story too? Just like I did, are you asking,

- How can I "join" God if I don't know where to find Him?
- How can I find a God I'm not sure I even believe in any more?

When you're in wilderness, you're not sure if God is real. When you're in wilderness, you haven't experienced God for so long you doubt His love, question the veracity of the Bible, and are tempted to think your season of faith was just a phase. You believe the whole "faith thing" was just a fairytale. Every time you thought God was working was probably coincidence. How does a believer who wants to reconnect with God but who is temporarily blind and deaf spiritually follow a God he or she can't see or hear?

Or maybe you're a new believer and haven't walked with God long enough to be sure you recognize Him or His work. Christians who are young in the faith want to follow God but are often unsure if what they are seeing or hearing is Him. It takes a while to develop an intimate relationship, and our relationship with our heavenly Father is no different. Getting to know one another requires spending time together, and if you're a new Christian, you're just beginning to spend quality time one-on-one with God.

Perhaps you've been a believer for some time but have never been "discipled" or taught to walk in the ways of faith. You prayed the prayer of salvation but then drifted along on your own. You're not a new believer, but you've also never matured because you haven't actively sought His knowledge and presence through Bible study and interactions with other Christians.

Whatever your circumstance, these are the important questions I want to help you find answers to:

- How can I put myself in a place where I can hear from God?
- How can I create an environment where God speaks to me?

- How can I open my eyes so I can see God?
- How can I learn to hear God?

If you're struggling to follow God, I have some great news for you. God, the "Hound of Heaven," is a seeing-eye dog! Even though we can't see Him, He never loses sight of us. *God pursues His children!* He is looking for you because He loves you. He gives special attention to those who have wandered away.[3] The pursuing God came and found me in my wilderness and led me, one yes at a time, into an interactive relationship with Him. [I share about the wilderness and the wonderful experience of God's love and pursuit in *From Faking It to Finding Grace* (Harvest House, 2005).] The pursuing God also finds us in our pre-belief state. He makes Himself known, draws us to Him, and gives us the opportunity to have a personal relationship with Him by inviting Him into our hearts and souls and lives through His Son, Jesus Christ. At the moment of our decision, God continues to pursue us throughout our earthly experience, convincing us of His love, convicting us of sin, connecting with our spirits so we experience Him in our day-to-day life, guiding us to fulfill our dreams.

God Provides When You Seek Him

When Gerry and I were living in California, we lived in campus housing for the first 18 months. In early December of Gerry's second year we left the campus area and moved two hours inland to Modesto so Gerry could pastor a church. He commuted to school for the next two-and-a-half years. The neighborhood near our church in Modesto was infested with crime. Our house was broken into and we were burgled, so we asked the detective who investigated the break-in how we could avoid it happening again. He gave us a one-word answer: "Move."

We could barely afford to live in this scary neighborhood, how would we finance "movin' on up"? Gerry and I began to actively listen and earnestly seek God. Because Gerry prefers to interact with God while moving (as opposed to being in a prayer closet), he began driving around our city, praying out loud for God to show him a way to keep his family safe. During one of those drives Gerry saw a half-acre lot with a lovely home and plenty of fruit trees for sale. He noticed a man in the yard, so pulled over to talk to him.

"Would you ever consider renting the place?" Gerry asked after spending a few minutes getting to know one another. And he did! This elderly, recently widowed homeowner wasn't ready in his heart to sell the "home place." If we would look after it for a while, he might be ready in a few years. And did I mention the hot tub out back? Because Gerry actively listened and earnestly sought God, God shocked the socks right off our feet!

And He will do the same thing for you! He did it with Moses. He did it with me. He can do it with you. You might argue that Moses (and I) weren't actively listening to or seeking God because we were on the "far side of the wilderness." Conversely, we both appeared (had you known me then) to be pursuing earthly interests and ignoring God. Moses was building up his flocks and herds while I repainted the inside of my house so many times I lost square footage. However, there is an "early version" of active listening and earnestly seeking I don't want you to miss—something I call "God-hunger."

God-hunger

During my years in spiritual wilderness I had an unfed hunger for God. I felt distant, removed, perhaps even abandoned by God. However, deep inside me there was a longing, a God-hunger. I don't know about you, but when I am hungry I eat. From my early teens until my 40s, I struggled to control my weight and was never able to lose that "last 10 pounds" that provided a little muffin top for my jeans. Then I read a book called *The Pritikin Weight Loss Breakthrough*[4] and it listed five principles to follow. I've forgotten three of them, but there are two I remember because they changed my life. Using my paraphrase, they are: 1) eat when you're hungry, but 2) only eat until you're satisfied.

Prior to reading this book I had forced myself to wait until mealtime, denying myself snacks even when I was really hungry. That caused extreme hunger, so by the time the meals finally arrived I stuffed myself. It was like storing up for a rainy day, only it never rained and my storehouse kept growing. Once I learned to eat as often as I wanted, even right at bedtime (formerly the ultimate no-no), I lost the extra pounds and have stayed at or near my goal weight for years now.

I think it's the same with spiritual hunger. I was holding out until the feast, thinking that God only reveals Himself in mighty acts of earth-shaking proportions. I scanned the horizon looking for that great big God. In reality, God was pursuing me with little snacks that I didn't let myself enjoy.

Can you relate? Is this your story right now? You want to be "satisfied with Jesus," as the old gospel hymn proclaims, but you are far from content with your relationship. When was the last time you saw Him in the sunset? When was the last time you heard Him in the kind words of a stranger? When was the last time you felt His embrace as you crawled into your comfortable and warm bed? *God is in every good thing you enjoy.* Are you recognizing Him? If not, ask Him to open your eyes, unstop your ears, and sharpen your senses. Admit you *are* hungry. Allow yourself to feel the pang of your God-hunger. And then put out your hand and let Him fill it with small and large glimpses of His glory. Every time He feeds you, thank Him. Nothing enhances a relationship like gratitude.

Perhaps you will be helped if you confess to one or two trusted friends the extent of your hunger. Ask them to pray for you and with you.

Embracing your God-hunger is the beginning of actively listening and earnestly seeking. Admitting you are hungry for God is noticing you're a work in process, and few of us like to be that vulnerable. We would rather give the impression we've got everything figured out:

> Much of our time is spent trying to create a persona that says, "I have it all together." And we go to great lengths to make sure that no one finds us lacking in any facet of our life. From our looks, to our careers, to our lifestyle, to our children, we want to be the whole package. We want to be the ones that others look to and say, "How do they pull it off?"[5]

Admitting your hunger opens the door to possibility. It expresses a need, and God responds to the expressed needs of His people. Over and over in the Old Testament, He hears the cries of His people and acts in response to those cries. The way He acts most often is to pursue one of His children and get them involved in the process. Abraham, Noah, Moses, Esther, Ruth, Deborah, Joshua, Jonah—these are just a few of the many God called to step out and get involved in bringing His solution people's problems. That's the way God still works. When you and I express our needs, God often responds by sending someone to help us, just as He sent Moses, Jonah, and others to people in their time who needed God. Often it is through the one He sends to you that He grabs your attention. And before long, when He knows we are ready, He uses us to bring hope and healing to people who need Him so they too can follow Him into freedom.

I have one caution to share: To hear God more clearly and understand His response to your honest heart-cry of God-hunger better, make sure you are close to His resources (His people, His community of faith). There is a corporate dimension to Christianity that is often misunderstood. God established the church to help His people encourage each other, lift each other up in prayer, serve Him, and reach out to people with the message of Jesus Christ. The Christian church provides a support system for Christ-followers and gives them unique experiences that build their faith and allow them to help others. Believers who choose to set themselves apart from an interdependent relationship with other believers might find it difficult to hear and understand all God has to say.[6] They may also be led astray more easily by people who want to give them false dreams and sway them against the Lord.

Repeatedly in my speaking and writing about spiritual dryness I stress the importance of people staying connected to a Bible-believing church. If you need to switch churches to find one you're more comfortable in, then do so rather than drop out altogether. If you do change, find a *smaller* one. Look for one where you won't get lost in the crowd. Find one where the pastor will soon know your name, where you will be comfortable enough to tell the pastor you are in a spiritual wilderness and have a hunger for God. If he tries to "fix" you, buy him a copy of *From Faking It to Finding Grace.* Ask him to pray for you.

Once you have admitted your need for God and expressed your God-hunger to someone else, the next step is to *ask, seek,* and *knock:*

Ask and it will be given to you; seek and you will find; knock and the door will be opened to you. For everyone who asks receives; he who seeks finds; and to him who knocks, the door will be opened (Matthew 7:7-8 NIV).

Ask by praying honestly:

God, I want to follow You and say yes to You, but I don't know where to find You. I want You to lead me, but You need to come after me because I don't know where You are. Please find me and give me a dream, and I will say yes to following Your lead.

God will answer that prayer!

You can actively *seek* by arranging your life so that you come into constant contact with God's teachings and His people. Join a Bible-study group. Tune in to preachers and teachers who adhere to biblical teachings on the radio or TV. Go to church. Have coffee with another believer. Read biographies of missionaries. Get involved in some kind of mission or ministry through your church. Watch for glimpses of God in your everyday life. Wait with expectation.

You can *knock* by not giving up. Never lose hope. Stay connected. Refuse to barricade yourself inside your comfort zone or medicate your senses with compulsive consumerism or unhealthy practices.

Be ready to be surprised because you may not recognize Him at first or be able to wrap your head around the dream He gives you when He answers your knock. Remember to answer, "Yes!"

God Habitat

Let's say you want to be able to identify birds by their sounds so that when you hear a certain series of chirps you can win friends (over 40) and influence people (especially other bird-watchers) by saying with confidence, "Oh, if I'm not mistaken, I believe that is the distinctive call of the Slaty-bellied Tesia." Before you can identify a wide range of birds you have to do a few things: buy or borrow a bird guidebook, make friends with other bird-watchers, go where birds are, watch and listen to birds.

Doesn't it seem foolish when people say they want to hear from God but they don't want to spend time in His guidebook (the Bible) or be anywhere near His habitat (church or where two or more believers are gathered in His name), or learn from other experienced God-watchers (believers)? This isn't rocket science; it's common sense. If you want to hear from God, make sure you're where people communicate with Him often. Go to places where you can catch sight of Him and His work in others. Hang around with people who know Him, love Him, and seek His ways. Find the most readable version of the Bible for you and read the four Gospels (Matthew, Mark, Luke, and John) over and over until Jesus "speaks" to you. When that happens, jot down what He says!

A dear friend gave me a tiny, lined journal bound with two carved wooden covers. I've had it for four years, and I've been filling it with many of the messages God has sent me through the Bible and other books I've read (religious and secular: remember, God can speak through anyone). God has used these to shape my life and the message He wants to send through me as I follow Him one yes at a time.

My "Rock" Encounter

My "rock" encounter with God took place at the kitchen table of a woman who was tuned in to God. Because I stayed involved in Christian community during my wilderness (I was a Christian leader's wife), I was surrounded by God's truths being lived out. I was around strong believers who prayed regularly. So this woman I was visiting told me she'd been led to pray for me for some time. (She didn't know I was in a prolonged season of spiritual drought. No one knew except Gerry and one or two very close friends.) She was praying for me because God asked her to and she said yes.

The wonderful story of this kitchen-table encounter that changed my life is told in greater detail in my book *From Faking It to Finding Grace*. The short version is that she invited me for tea, during which time she revealed the message (the dream) God had put on her heart to share with me. Opening her Bible to Psalm 51, she read it and exhorted me using the words of the psalmist David. When she reached verse 13: "Then I will teach transgressors your ways, and sinners will turn back to you," she paused, looked up and told me that was God's dream for me.[7]

In her eyes it was clear and quite simple. My job was to teach transgressors (people who don't know God, who live outside His truths, or who are spiritually wandering) and point them to Jesus Christ. Since I was already a local newspaper journalist and a columnist for a popular Christian family magazine, she probably assumed I would do this teaching and correcting through writing. What she didn't know at the time was my "big secret"—I *was* one of those transgressors!

Easy for You

What appeared simple to this Christian woman sent to help me seemed terribly complex and confusing to me. How could a person of such little faith (me! In fact, I questioned whether I had any faith left) teach others anything meaningful about God? My friend's prophetic words were ludicrous. However, when she prayed aloud for me, I had a sense of a spiritual presence that was so palpable I didn't want to open my eyes after she said "Amen," fearing "it" would disappear like a genie in a bottle. That "presence" was God! The One I had once experienced but had lost touch with. Oh how I missed Him! Oh how I hungered for Him.

I opened my eyes and, as expected, He was gone. I left my friend's home with mixed feelings. The dark hopelessness that had been shadowing me for years suddenly was pierced by a tiny pinprick of light. A dream had been planted even though it seemed impossible. Walking over the crisp snow on that cold winter day, I prayed the first real prayer I'd prayed for a long time:

> Okay, God, if You are real and if You are who she says You are, I will "teach transgressors and bring sinners back." I will say yes to following You. But You're going to have to come after me because I don't know where to find You.

I had thrown down the gauntlet that God had been waiting for years to see. He was poised with a response.

Out of the Blue

I didn't think of my friend's words again until days, weeks, maybe even months later when, out of the blue, the phone rang. It was some-one I'd never met requesting that I come and speak at a women's week-end retreat in Ontario (Canada), two time zones east of my Alberta home. Since I'd done very little public speaking up to that point, my first reaction was to politely refuse. What could I possibly say in my spiritually dry condition that would justify their expense and expec-tations? But before I refused out loud, my mind flashed back to that encounter at my friend's kitchen table and my prayer on the walk home. *What about that spark of a dream in my heart that I might "know" God again?* I wondered. *Is this God's response to my request for Him to come after me?* As the words "You're going to have to come after me" danced across my mind. I had promised God that I would say yes. And now here I was, phone in hand, being asked to "teach transgressors and bring sinners back."

Thinking I must be crazy but not wanting to miss out if this really was God's way of coming after me, I said the first yes to following Him in a long time. I hung up the phone and exclaimed, "Am I nuts? What am I doing?" But I'm here to tell you that I wasn't nuts. I was, at last, being obedient. Over the next few years, I followed God out of my spir-itual wilderness one yes at a time.

There is an important element I learned the hard way, and I don't want you to miss it. It's difficult to hear from God if you're not follow-ing Him. It's so easy to get so caught up in the world and what's hap-pening that you simply miss God's voice…or misunderstand Him. The antidote? If you are at the place where you've admitted your God-hunger and kept yourself in God habitat—voila! You are probably more tuned in to hearing Him. And when you sense the dream He has for you and you're ready to say yes, embark! You'll find it *gets easier to hear Him* when you get moving.

When God points you in a certain direction, *say yes with your feet.* One *simple, immediate, possible* yes leads to another, and another, as you obey His directives and attain your dreams. Move forward even if it looks like the water won't hold you (like Peter stepping out of the boat), even if you're not sure where you'll end up (like Abraham when he left Ur), and even if it looks like it doesn't make sense (like Abraham about to sacrifice Isaac). When you move, you'll begin to hear Him more clearly. Why? One simple reason: You have put yourself in a place where you can't make it without Him. You need Him now to pursue and realize His and your dream. This "active need" sharpens your spiritual hearing. The absolutely best place to hear from God is while you're moving forward to achieve the dream because you are in the center of His will.

What's Next

Let's review:

- *God pursues His children.* He comes looking for you because He loves you. He gives special attention to those who have wandered away.[8]
- *He grabs your attention.* From burning bushes to pizza boxes, God will do what it takes to catch your eye.[9]
- *He gives you a dream.* He points you in the direction He wants you to go.[10]
- *Say yes with your feet.* One simple, immediate, possible step after another, follow God one yes at a time.[11]

The next two points we're going to explore are what will help us be persistent and motivated as we pursue the dreams God gives us:

- *He sends proofs to keep you on track.* The divine incentives of His peace, His power, and His provision are recognizable assurances that God is real, that you're on the right path, that will help you battle discouragement, and that will keep you moving forward.
- *He is your reward.* God is the great I Am who loves you. He wants you to experience His presence. As it was with Joshua, whose job it was to "take" the Promised Land, God's "I Am" presence is what overcomes the barriers that try to impede or halt your progress.[12]

PART 2

PROOFS

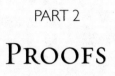

6

CHOCOLATES

*When the Spirit prompts you to leave a Circle of Comfort,
walk across a room, and enter the Zone of the Unknown
to discover someone's story, he wants you to show up,
not someone you think you are supposed to be.* [1]

BILL HYBELS

G od loves you and has a plan for your life. As a Christian, you probably also know, as the old hymn says, that the best way to be "happy in Jesus, is to trust and obey." [2] Jesus said, "If you love Me, you will keep My commandments" (John 14:15). To keep yourself motivated and on target toward your dream by following God one yes at a time, a great strategy is to look for and appreciate the divine incentives God gives to encourage you. I call these *proofs* of God.

Some friends of mine love hiking. They were born and raised in Germany, but they have traveled all over the world by working on cruise ships as young adults. They hiked on their days off every time the ship docked. They settled at long last in Calgary, Alberta, so they could be close to the endless source of hiking trails in the Canadian Rockies. When they were nearing 40, they had two babies in two years, but they kept right on hiking by packing them on their backs. When the toddlers grew too heavy to carry, they decided to train them to hike. After much coaxing, crying, and eventually carrying, they tried getting the children into hiking but they wound up cutting their hikes short and turning back in frustration. Finally they came up with a plan.

Along with the extra socks, bug repellant, sunscreen, moleskin, hats, rain capes, healthy snacks, and water, they added a bag of individually wrapped chocolates. On the next hike, daddy jogged ahead a short distance and put two chocolates on the trail and then came back. He and mommy then played a counting game with the kids. "Fifty steps to the chocolate!" they'd say to encourage the kids. Their initial hikes were short—no more than "four chocolates worth" (they were also health nuts). Chocolate-by-chocolate little "Hansel and Gretel" learned to love hiking. Their parents subtly began putting the chocolates farther and farther apart until finally they only gave them as a reward once they reached their destination and ate their lunches. They always made sure to factor in enough time at the hike's destination to thoroughly enjoy what they had traveled to see.

Chocolates on the Trail

God does that for us too. As a loving Father, He shows us the path He wants us to take and makes sure the first step is within our means. He waits for us to say yes and step forward and begin walking; He places incentives at intervals along our path to encourage us to continue walking with Him. The primary incentive is having Him as our "hiking companion"! His presence gives us peace and power, and His provision ensures we have everything we need for the journey. And like my German friends did, He gradually moves the "chocolates" farther apart when He knows we are mature enough to go a little longer without a treat or reward.

God in His wisdom knew that a key component of my recovery from spiritual drought was confession by sharing where I was really at. The "confessional" was quite a bit bigger than what I expected mind you. God's plan was for me to publicly admit to my decade of wilderness travel so other wanderers would find hope, comfort, and direction for renewal. He started by giving me a dream to "more fully experience God." I wanted to see Him, to hear from Him, to sense His presence, to feel His embrace, to know His will—all the things I had once known but had lost somewhere along my meandering life journey. Once the dream was firmly planted in my heart, God clearly showed me the first step: saying yes to an invitation to speak.

He used that first speaking experience to convince me I could do it. So when a second invitation came on the heels of the first, I had the courage to say yes again. While I was preparing for my second event I suddenly understood that the purpose for which I was called was to be honest about my spiritual dryness. This was a message few (if anyone) in the Christian community was carrying, but something I suspected many believers might be secretly struggling with. As the wife of a national Christian leader in Canada, the last thing I wanted to do was publicly admit the truth about something as bewildering and shameful (in my eyes) as my decade in the wilderness. And God knew that. But He also knew that was a step I needed to take to move into spiritual renewal.

Stepping Out in Dryness

That first phone call inviting me to speak was the beginning of many calls and emails from people who found me and requested that I speak at their Christian events. I didn't advertise, didn't use my husband's very recognizable last name (I used my maiden name), didn't get listed in the phone book, didn't have any training, and was completely unknown, and still people wanted me to speak. So it was obvious even to one with as little faith as I had that God *must be* involved. I was shocked that God wanted me to step out and bring hope to other spiritually dried-up Christians *even though I was still dry myself.* What I didn't recognize at the time was that it was no different than one recovering alcoholic reaching out to another recovering alcoholic. The relationship benefits *both* parties. God knew the way to restore my faith was to put me in a place where I couldn't live without Him. He invited me to say yes to a life I couldn't live without Him, a path that had to be walked *by faith.*

To walk this trail He put me on, I would need Him every step of the way. I would also need lots of "chocolates" in the early going to convince me that I was, indeed, on the right path. The "rewards" were hearing from God, who had been invisible to me for years, and traveling. And God didn't hold back. In my first two years of speaking I was invited to speak in places as exotic as Grand Cayman Island and

Norway. Talk about pretty hefty chocolates—I'm talking a full-sized chocolate Easter bunny! I'd always wanted to see the world but had never been able to do it. Now I was being paid to travel.

I also spoke from coast to coast in Canada and made several forays into the United States. Then slowly and subtly, as I was ready, God began to change the flavor of those chocolates. Instead of blessing me with exotic locations, He sent me to every backwoods way station in Christendom. The "incentives" or *proofs* of God's presence I needed most were given to me—hundreds of tear-stained, hurting sinners like me sharing their stories and hugs and meaningful interactions with God. I sensed His presence more often. The Bible began to speak to my heart again. I was praying more often. Cynicism waned. I recognized His work in others. The rewards of His presence, His peace, His power, and His provision are what sustains me now as I continue to say yes to following Him.

The Chocolates Keep Coming

The chocolates continue to come in the form of God's love and presence and inspirational words, thoughtful cards, meaningful gifts from people whose lives have been touched by my message. I've also received bookmarks with encouraging Scripture verses and delight in my new friends who live in faraway places. These blessings help me continue to say yes to God.

Am I saying we should only follow God because He gives rewards? What about the people who followed Jesus and died as martyrs? Where were their "chocolates"? That's a good question. You and I will also die one day, and our deaths could involve horrible suffering. But regardless of how we die, I believe that while we live God gives us what we need to keep following Him. The men and women in the Bible received blessings as they followed God one yes at a time too. Wasn't Isaac Abraham's reward? And what about the ram caught in the thicket that was a replacement sacrifice for Isaac? Wasn't that a blessing? God places many rewards (blessings, incentives, *proofs*) in the paths of those who follow Him.

What about you? Are you seeing the chocolates He is placing on your trail? If you are, keep hiking. If you are not, ask Him to open your eyes. If there are no chocolates, you may have wandered off the trail He wants you to be on. Trust me—I know how easy it is to start out following God and somehow lose your way. You can get back on God's path by talking to Him and listening intently to His guidance.

God Proves Himself to Gideon

There's a guy who makes his Bible debut in the sixth chapter of Judges. When we first meet Gideon he is threshing wheat, so we know he's probably a farmer or at least the son of a farmer. An "Angel of the LORD" appears to Gideon and calls him a "mighty warrior."[3] We don't know if Gideon had prior military experience or if God was simply setting him up for what He would say next. Then God offered him a dream. It was what Gideon wanted more than anything else—freedom from the desert raiders who, on their swift camels, had plundered and destroyed the Israelites' crops for seven years, throwing them into poverty. There's only one catch: Gideon would have to go out and fight the Midianites. And considering that he was hiding when the angel found him, we can assume Gideon wasn't much of a fighter.[4]

Gideon's response sounds just like something I'd say: "If the LORD is with us, why has all this happened? And where are all His wonders that our fathers told us about?"[5] Gideon was probably soaked with sweat, itchy with chaff, and frustrated beyond belief by trying to thresh wheat in an airless pit without the necessary breeze to separate the kernel from the chaff. He may have been having trouble separating his anger against the enemy who had forced him into this pit and the God who didn't seem to care that he was in it.

The angel of the Lord tells Gideon, "Go *in the strength you have* and deliver Israel from the power of Midian."[6] Gideon asks, "How can I deliver Israel?"[7] Just like we do, Gideon thinks the *strength he has* isn't enough. So often when God gives us a dream, our first thought is to think there are more qualified, gifted, mature, well-known, proven, resourceful, battle-seasoned, experienced, respected people who could achieve the dream so why is He asking me? Have you noticed that God has a habit of picking people who don't think they can do what He asks them to do? Why is that? My theory is that God does that to guarantee that the one He's chosen will ask for and follow His guidance closely. He picks someone who knows he or she can't accomplish the task alone. So God tells Gideon what He told Abraham and Moses and all His other followers, including you and me: "I will be with you."[8]

Hot Chocolate!

God gives Gideon the dream (picture-promise), but Gideon has to follow Him to get the steps (plan). Every big dream is accomplished one decision at a time. The "yeses" Gideon says are laid out in the sixth through eighth chapters of Judges. Before Gideon makes the first move, he wants some *proof.* He asks the angel to give him a sign.[9] He wants to be sure his dream is from God and not some crazy notion from who knows where. Gideon is looking for some kind of chocolate on the trail to let him know he's on the right path. The angel causes fire to come from the rock on which Gideon's offering was placed. The offering was consumed—hot chocolate!

Emboldened by the sign, Gideon follows God. It is significant that the next order from the angel and Gideon's first step of obedience, while not easy, was *simple:* He was given instructions to get his father's young bull and another one, tear down his father's altar of Baal and the Asherah pole, and use them as fuel for a proper sacrifice.[10] This first step was *immediate.* Judges 6:25 says, "On that very night." And this first step was *possible,* although Gideon made a slight adjustment. Being too afraid to tear down the idols in daylight, Gideon waits until nightfall to carry out the task. (Destroying the altars was punishable by death.)[11]

White Chocolate!

Gideon's next step is to send messengers throughout the land to gather an army. But Gideon wants to be assured once again that the dream is from God and not his own hare-brained delusion brought on by heat stroke from too much pit threshing. This is when the famous sheepskin "fleece" tests happen. Gideon lays out a fleece two times, asking God to first make it soaking wet with dew but leaving the ground dry, and second to make the fleece dry with dew on the ground all around it. God comes through exactly as requested. White chocolate! Gideon knows he's on the right path.

Gideon moves forward in faith to take the next step. His messengers amass an impressive army of 32,000 recruits. Gideon is going to need every one of them because the enemy is so numerous they are described as a "swarm of locusts."[12] But God tells Gideon to send the men who were afraid home. So 22,000 men scamper back to their tents and herds. God isn't finished! He tells Gideon to further reduce his fighting force by conducting a drinking test down by the river. Everyone who puts down his weapon, lies down and laps the water like a dog stays. All the others are sent home.

At the end of the day, Gideon had an army of only 300 men. I'm sure Gideon was glad he started the preparations with the fleece tests because following the directions to trim down his army had to seem like folly. God's reasoning for reducing the army by such a huge proportion was so that Israel would not be able to brag, "I did it myself."[13] Don't miss this incredible truth because God still works this way in your life and mine. He calls us to live in a way we can't without Him. He gives us dreams we can't fulfill without following Him one yes at a time.

Dark Chocolate!

The next step for Gideon is to go into the enemy's camp. The Lord tells him if he is afraid to take his servant Purah and go at night to listen to their chatter. Once there Gideon hears a man describe the puzzling dream he had the previous night. The man's friend interprets the dream to mean that the sword of Gideon will conquer them. Dark chocolate! Encouraged, Gideon goes back to his 300 men, divides them into three groups and gives them explicit instructions: surround the enemy camp, wait for his signal, blow the trumpets, break the pitchers, hold the torches high, and shout: "The sword of the LORD and of Gideon!"[14] The Israelites do as they are told, and the enemy flees in terror. Their leaders are killed and the oppression ends. Peace returns to the land.

I have used the metaphor of chocolates on the trail to represent God's assurance to His followers that they have correctly heard from Him and are walking in the way He wants them to. The "chocolates" are very helpful in encouraging those who are young in their faith or have lost their way. They help them follow a clearly marked trail, kind of like Hansel and Gretel following crumbs to find their way home. God has other ways of letting us know we are following as we should too. These *proofs* are the palpable *presence, peace, power,* and *provision* of God when we are following Him and fulfilling His *picture-promise* (dream). We're going to take a closer look at these "p" words.

7

PEACE

As people develop a relationship with God,
he doesn't encapsulate them in protective bubbles;
he arms them for battle. [1]

I'm an image consultant," she answered. No surprise there. We were the first two people to be seated at a large round table at a women's event where I was the keynote speaker. The woman beside me didn't know who I was yet. And after hearing what her business was, I wasn't sure I wanted to confess mine. Secretly I hoped she'd figure it out by looking at me. She didn't.

Her image said "*Grrr.*" Her hair was as elaborate as a warrior's feathered headdress worn for battle or victory celebrations. Her war paint was precisely applied, and her lips were the color of fresh blood after a kill. She was draped in layers of black with a leopard print scarf coiled around her neck. Her voice was modulated and sure. Each word was carefully chosen and delivered like an arrow to the mark. Suddenly I felt like prey.

Isn't it amazing how even innocent bystanders can look like terrorists when our minds are clouded by fear? This lovely woman took on the persona of the enemy as I allowed my lack of confidence, poor self-image, and fear to color my thinking. The bravado I'd carried into the room scurried for cover, leaving me vulnerable to attack. The barrier of comparison went up faster than yellow crime scene tape, interfering with my ability to hear God. Anything He was saying to calm my fear or bring me peace was muffled behind the sound barrier I'd thrown up. Since I wasn't keen on hearing a critique of *my* image, I steered the conversation away from me by asking another question: "So what is the most common mistake people make?"

The Right Image

"Nails," she responded without hesitation. I slipped my hands, already in my lap, deep under the overhanging tablecloth. Her scarlet talons were in plain view. I'd seen shower doors with less acrylic. "People don't realize how important the details are," she continued. "A flawless manicure makes a statement."

"You are so right!" I agreed, keeping my "flawed statements" inside my fists and hidden beneath the tablecloth. Natural, flimsy, peeling, and stubby, my nails were still recovering from two years of wearing acrylics. I'd loved those fake nails because they bolstered my confidence. I loved to click them on tabletops. I draped my hands across visible surfaces like a newly engaged woman hoping to draw attention to her bling. I'd worn acrylics with pride, shaking hands with everyone who glanced my way, patting the arms of complete strangers, laying my hands in open view like jewelry in a top-of-the-line boutique. Recently, however, God had revealed a new dream for those hands of mine.

Working Hands

My idea had been to allow my natural nails to breathe a little during my two-month speaking break, and then to have another full set of confidence-boosters applied before hitting the road again. Meanwhile, I was invited to join the "Girls Nite Out" team as one of their speakers.[2] I was told that part of this evening of "fun, faith and fellowship" involved a brief appeal for people to sponsor a child through World Vision. This gave me pause. How could I ask others to sponsor a needy child if I weren't a World Vision child sponsor myself? So as I prayerfully considered saying yes to joining their team, I asked World Vision to send me information on child sponsorship. The day their envelope arrived I pulled out six information packets containing photos of children waiting to be chosen. I spread the photos out on my kitchen table and read their stories. My heart was so tugged by the overwhelming need. How was I going to decide which one to sponsor?

Placing my hands on the table, fingers spread-eagled so I could touch every little face, I asked God to show me which child to choose. *Which one? Which one?* I prayed as my eyes walked from face to face. All at once the children slipped out of focus, and I saw only my hands. I stared at the not-so-pretty natural nails I was planning to upgrade in a few days. A dollar sign and a number splashed across my mind. The cost of maintaining one set of acrylic nails equaled the cost of sponsoring two children. *Which deserved my money?* Two hands...or two kids? The choice was obvious. One *simple, immediate, possible* yes later, I chose two kids and canceled my next nail appointment. I've never made another one.

Denying Christ Takes Many Forms

Seated beside the image consultant just weeks after swapping my fake nails for two kids who had been orphaned by AIDS, I couldn't bring myself to tell her why I thought my homely hands were beautiful in their own way, that I had a strong case for making a powerful statement *with* flawed nails. Minutes before I had been proud of my hands because I was allowing God to use them for something good. Now I was hiding them under the table linen in shame. The vision of Jesus looking across a smoky courtyard at Peter in the predawn chill flew into my head. Denying Christ takes many forms. Shaking my head like an Etch-a-Sketch to erase the imagined face of a disappointed Jesus Christ, I continued to play the journalist. I asked my seatmate every question I could think of until the program began. My stomach was in knots as my familiar old enemy, the saboteur, crept in and took aim. He had a clear shot because I had allowed fear to throw up a barrier between my greatest ally (God) and me.

Let the Show Begin

The evening began with a fashion show. The models stepped, stopped, swiveled, and sashayed up and down the long runway that jutted deep into the large room filled with the din of hundreds of gals enjoying an evening fueled by chocolate, caffeine, and momentary freedom from the cares of jobs and kids.

After rousing music by a talented band that got everyone on their feet and hollering for more, the emcee launched into a flowery introduction of the keynote speaker: "Connie Cavanaugh is screamingly funny…you'll be slapping your knees…you'll be rolling in the aisles… you'll die laughing…." Her innocent enthusiasm inched the bar, notch by notch, up to unreachable levels. By the time she finally called me onstage, Bill Cosby would have had to dig deep to meet the expectations implanted in those women.

So You Think You're Funny, Eh?

Flicking the toggle for the lapel mike to on, I charged up the steps to the stage and launched into my welcoming remarks. No one heard me. My words fwooped, plopped, and trickled about three feet, like a topped golf ball. The mike wasn't working. Setting my notes on the podium, I detached the power pack from my belt and checked. The green light was illuminated, but my voice wasn't being amplified. Precious seconds ticked by as the audience waited for me to get aisle-rolling hilarity going.

The sound technician, miles away at the back of the room signaled for me to pick up the microphone at the back corner of the stage. It was well out of the spotlight and not wireless. I've seen safety conscious teakettles with longer cords. My plan to walk out onto the runway and get close to the people went *poof*.

Tethered in a dim corner, removed from my audience by acres of empty runway, wearing last year's fashions, and waving hands that made a statement—but not the "right" one, I forgot my opening line and had to glance at my notes. The words literally danced on the page before my eyes. It was like trying to read Sanskrit on a jumping bean. I couldn't focus. My knees were so shaky I was thankful that last year's fashions were stovepipe legs! My tongue stuck to the roof my mouth. My hands shook as I tried to juggle the microphone, arrange my notes on a flimsy music stand, and battle my rising panic.

Punch lines that usually drew riotous laughter produced sporadic lip twitches and twisted smiles that never blossomed into full grins. No knees were slapped. No bodies were doubled over in joyful pain. The only one in pain was the speaker as I endured the longest labor of my life that didn't produce a baby at the end.

A Two-cent Tip

Back at my table after polite applause I fought the urge to run from the room, find the nearest highway, and stick out my thumb. I was 1500 miles from home but would have gladly started walking that night. Time stood still as I smiled and nodded and talked to people, few of whom opted to buy my book so they could take a little piece of me home with them. It reminded me of the day I found a two-cent tip on one of my tables the summer I was a waitress in a tourist town in British Columbia. I got the message.

An eternity passed before I got back to my hotel. It was almost midnight. I was humiliated, emotionally exhausted, alone, and scared. I knew that the next morning I had another event in a nearby city, and somehow I needed to find the courage to walk up on stage again. I wanted to quit but I knew I couldn't...and wouldn't. Like Gideon and his fleece, I needed proof that I was on the right path. Was speaking God's dream for me or my deluded ambitions.

When Will It End?

It had been a full year since my last bout of severe stage fright, and I had assumed I was finally over it. This was the longest break between panic episodes I'd experienced. Tonight's debacle proved otherwise. Alone in my room, far from the comforts of husband and home, propped up in bed with only the light of the bedside lamp to fend off the darkness that wanted to consume me, I cried out to God, "How long, Lord?"

By this time I had been traveling and speaking for about nine years. It's natural and common for speakers to feel nervous before they get up to speak, but I was often terrified. Mindful of the fact that any platform is a great privilege and that, like the apostle Paul, I knew I was the worst of sinners, every time I approached a podium I felt a huge burden of responsibility to represent Christ with integrity. I knew part of my panic problem was that I hadn't yet accepted that the way God made me was exactly who He wanted me to be onstage and off.

I was, am, and always will be a storyteller. I love a good tale. I come from a long line of Irish word weavers. Stories don't just illustrate a point for me. Often the story *is* the point. People remember stories. I believe that's why Jesus told so many parables. He wanted His listeners to remember God's teachings, and stories help do that by making memorable associations. It took me almost a decade of speaking before God overcame my presupposition that said: *If something comes natural to me, it probably isn't good enough* (the *comparison* barrier). During the beginning of my speaking career I was constantly frustrated because no matter how hard I tried to be a serious Bible teacher, believing that was the only godly approach, I kept defaulting to funny stories. I was having a hard time reconciling who I was by God's design with who I thought a Christian speaker should be.

The Family Flaw

Some speaking events were more difficult than others, and audience size seemed to have little to do with it. For years I didn't figure out what triggered my panic attacks. I simply chalked them up to genetics. Anxiety and agoraphobia don't *run* in our family, they *gallop*. I prayed for healing and help. Slowly things improved and my bouts of mindboggling panic got further and further apart as I racked up air miles. But I longed for the day when I didn't have to fear the figurative sniper's bullet as I walked onstage. In most cases the way I was able to rise above my fear, calm the shakes, unstick my tongue from the roof of my mouth, and slow down my racing heart was by telling a funny story. Within minutes I would be laughing along with the audience and fear would be gone.

But that episode at the women's event with the fashion show was the worst I'd ever known. Unrelenting and fierce, I felt powerless from the hello to the amen. By the time I crawled into bed that night I was convinced I wasn't able to do what God had called me to do or be the person I thought He wanted me to be. So downhearted I didn't even know how to pray, I propped up the pillows and reached for my Bible.

Bible Roulette

Hoping to find peace but not sure where to look, I flipped open to the book of Galatians. Paul was my current favorite Bible guy. Chapter 1 began on the right-hand page of my Bible, but my eyes caught a highlighted phrase midway down the left-hand page. In the twelfth chapter of 2 Corinthians, verse 7, I read, "So that I would not exalt myself, a thorn in the flesh was given to me, a messenger of Satan to torment me so I would not exalt myself."[3] *That's what this stage fright is!* I thought. *A thorn!* Reading Paul's words gave me the comfort of knowing I wasn't the only one. Misery *does* love company.

This passage wasn't new to me, but I hadn't connected Paul's thorn to my panic. I read on, hoping Paul would tell me what to do. "Concerning this, I pleaded with the Lord three times to take it away from me. But He said to me, 'My grace is sufficient for you, for power is perfected in weakness.'"[4] Even though Paul asked God repeatedly for his thorn to be removed, it was not. This wasn't what I wanted to hear. But right on the heels of that was God's response to Paul's request, basically saying, "I won't remove your thorn, but I'll give you the grace to live with it." And Paul's response to that was amazing:

> Therefore, I will most gladly boast all the more about my weaknesses, so that Christ's power may reside in me. So because of Christ, I am pleased in weaknesses, in insults, in catastrophes, in persecutions, and in pressures. For when I am weak, then I am strong.[5]

Weaknesses, catastrophes, pressures. How could Paul be pleased in those things? I certainly wasn't. I was humiliated, terrified, and ashamed. I had been exceedingly weak earlier tonight and I still felt that way. I prayed, "Lord, am I doing what You want me to do? Am I on the right path?" I needed proof.

His Presence

I reread Paul's words and noticed that "so that I would not exalt myself" appeared twice in verse 7. *God doesn't want me to miss this. It's not about me,* I thought. *He never said it would be easy, just simple. Follow*

Me. This path He has me on is one I can't walk alone. I need Him. My need for Him forces me to stick close. And He is telling me His grace is sufficient for me because His power is perfected in my weakness.

If power is perfected in weakness, I'm perfect for God. I laughed. Weakness? I had a great supply. As God's peace washed over me, I realized that I had come to His Word looking for some kind of fix just like I open the door of the medicine cabinet when in search of something to stop a headache. I soon realized Jesus doesn't just *have* enough; He *is* enough. The words of Paul were my Lord's words whispered into my soul. The sense of God's presence was so real it was a fragrance surrounding me. He was letting me know my weakness wasn't a problem as long as I followed Him *one*—and only one—yes at a time. I didn't have to answer for my entire future, only for tomorrow morning. Would I say yes? If I believed His grace *was* sufficient I would say yes. And I did. His peace that really does "transcend all understanding" came over me.[6] When we say yes, God *proves* Himself with His presence and peace.

Closing my eyes to pray and eventually sleep, I said, "Lord, Your grace is sufficient for right now and for tomorrow too. Forgive me for my fear and my doubt. I'll go tomorrow, and if I get another panic attack, I guess You'll just have to get me through it like You did tonight. Thank You. Amen." And then I slept.

Here We Go Again

At breakfast the following morning I was amazed to learn from my traveling companions that while I certainly hadn't hit any homers the previous night, no one but me had been aware of the extent of my panic. That knowledge helped—a little. But when I got to the venue for that day's event, I was once again consumed with fear. Sitting in the front row waiting my turn to speak, I bowed my head and prayed while wiping my teary eyes. *This isn't supposed to be about me, Lord!* I cried in my heart. *How can I focus on bringing hope to others when I am so helpless and terrified and focused on me?*

"When I am weak, then I am strong," I heard deep within my soul. God's presence was palpable. My heart-cry had broken through fear's barrier. I had access to Him—to His peace. Still shaking, I stepped up to the microphone and started telling one of my favorite funny stories. I must think I'm funny because before too long I was laughing as hard as the audience was. I never noticed when the shaking with fear changed to shaking with mirth. God's grace was, is, and always will be sufficient. His peace? Priceless.

Why Do We Follow God?

Ask anyone why he or she follows God, and you might hear, "to be part of His work on earth, to make a difference in the world, to make my life count for something, to be involved in something bigger than me." Such noble notions are true, but they are only part of the story. As much as altruism drives us to make the world a better place, deep inside we are also driven by our own needs. We want to feel loved, to overcome fear, to salve our loneliness, to heal our brokenness, and to find happiness.

The reason most of us say yes to following God is because we want to sense His presence because that's what brings us peace, gives us access to power, sends us provision, and energizes us to go after His dreams for us. The reason I said yes to my God-inspired dream and began publicly telling my wilderness story was to get close to Him. If that meant I had to be honest about my biggest secret I was willing to do it. If others were helped and encouraged along the way that was awesome, but what I really cared about in the beginning was primarily me and my relationship with God. And guess what? God knew that. He's smart. That's why the first "chocolates" He placed along my path were me-oriented (paid trips to exotic locations). Before long the flavor of those chocolates changed because God had begun to change me, to mature me spiritually. He instilled in me a love for the people whose feet He sent me to wash. Over time the chocolates changed again and became words and hugs and tears and smiles from people whose lives were impacted because I was saying yes to God.

Yes, I was a little surprised that God kept leading me through so much terrifying terrain year after year as I continued to speak publicly. I battled the same problems that had backed me into the wilderness (fear, shame, pride, guilt, comparison, doubt) and provided me with bricks to erect barriers to keep God out of my comfortable world. I often second-guessed myself as well as His dream for me. I needed constant proof—lots of chocolates on the trail—to keep me moving forward on the path He designed for me.

Eventually I matured enough spiritually that I could follow God in spite of my weakness. Better yet, weakness was good because it kept me needing Him. And best of all, I am learning that no matter what my weaknesses, there really is only one answer—Jesus. By His grace we have the power to overcome our barriers.

Yes by Yes

As I continued to follow God yes by yes, I found myself signing letters, emails, books, and cards with a new phrase that just popped into my head: *Keep following God one yes at a time.* It dawned on me that God had led me out of my decade of spiritual dryness *one yes at a time.* And He was continuing to lead me in my post-wilderness life one yes at a time. As I thought back to my early days of vibrant faith, I realized I had followed Him one yes at a time then too. In fact, the only time He hadn't led me one yes at a time was during my wilderness time when I stopped saying yes to Him and lost my way. Maybe following Him one yes at a time was the answer for more than just my panic episodes. Maybe it was the answer for everything that tried to hold me back from living the dreams He had for me.

A Final Word About Peace

"Peace" is the *acceptance* of who you are in the midst of your weakness and the *assurance* that God is sufficient. Peace is the emotional state that comes from complete dependence on Him in the present moment and circumstance. Peace is not just the absence of turmoil or the removal of anxiety-causing circumstances. Peace is the sense of God's palpable presence in the midst of those things. "The peace of God, which transcends all understanding, will guard your hearts and your minds in Christ Jesus."[7] Because His peace "guards our hearts" we don't need the barriers we put up to "guard our hearts." Every time we say yes and follow Him, He helps us deconstruct our barriers. Mine is fear; yours might be pride. Mine is doubt; yours might be self-righteousness. Mine is shame; yours might be legalism. There are all types of barriers, but they all come down the same way—one yes at a time.

The "rest of the story" about my stage fright is that I have never had another panic attack of that caliber. And I hope I never will again. Does that mean God removed my thorn even though He didn't remove Paul's? I don't know. All I know is I have an endless supply of other "thorns" that drive me to God to ask for His sufficiency. Perhaps in His mercy He knew I could live without severe stage fright. The healing for my panic was tightly interwoven with my acceptance of *my sufficiency* as well as His. What I mean is that there is also peace in *accepting who you are and allowing God to use you exactly as He made you*. I no longer battle my natural bent, but thank Him for giving me the gifts I have. I use those gifts for His glory.

You might think that what you have to use for Him isn't quite up to par. You think you're not godly enough, not spiritual enough, not serious enough, not sweet enough, not kind enough, not sure enough, not smart enough, not bold enough, not educated enough, or not experienced enough. All of those "not enoughs" are barriers that hold you back from the dreams God has for you.

Jesus, whose power is perfected in weakness, is dying (has died, in fact) to demonstrate His grace through your faithfulness. And remember, faithfulness is simply saying yes with your feet. Don't worry about changing your image. Just say yes and let Him fine-tune you as you follow Him.

8

POWER

*I pray that He may grant you, according to the
riches of His glory, to be strengthened with power
through His Spirit in the inner man.*

EPHESIANS 3:16

D o you need regular assurances from God that He is real and personal? That He is who He says He is in the Bible? I think most
believers do. We are comforted, encouraged, even emboldened by the
proofs God sends when He knows we need a sign. That word, "sign," has
many layers of meaning in the Bible. Some are good, some not so good.

I once took a vanload of women on a nine-hour drive. It should
have only taken three hours, but unfortunately I didn't pay attention
to the signs. A sign is a "symbol, action or occurrence that points to
something beyond itself," such as the signs I missed that pointed the
way to the city the women and I were trying to reach.[1] That was many
years ago, and I still get teased about that road trip.

In the Old Testament, signs were used for many things, including
referring to miraculous interventions of God, such as His parting of the
Red Sea so the Israelites could cross.[2] In the New Testament, sign "can
refer to a natural event, but more often it refers…to a miraculous act
authenticating God's activity."[3] The meaning I want to focus on is that
"signs can be a verification of the presence and power of God at work
in circumstances or in His people."[4] When we sense His presence and
see His power at work in us or around us, it is a welcome sign that He
is who He says He is and He can do what He says He can do.

Because the word "sign" was given a bad reputation by Jesus when He accused people of following Him only because He fed them and He called the Scribes and Pharisees an "evil and adulterous generation" when they asked for a sign, I prefer the word "proof" to describe what happens when God lets us know He is real and personally involved in the details of our lives.[5] The best proof, because it is the difference between "knowing there is a God" and "knowing God," is His palpable presence. Sensing His presence proves He's real and alive today, not just a myth we cling to from long ago. Along with His presence comes peace. When peace washes over us in the midst of our storms, God proves Himself to us in a tangible way. He is able, He is near, He is sufficient, He is aware of what we are going through, and so much more. Another proof God graces us with is His power. As we follow Him, He occasionally calls us to do things we can't do in our own strength. Our acts of obedience—saying yes with our feet—do two things: They "prove" our faith and invite God to release His power in the situation.

In his gospel, John uses the word "sign" instead of "miracle" because he sees the signs as pointing to the reality of who Jesus is. When people see His signs (miracles) Jesus expects them to be strengthened in their faith and to know that He is God.[6] That is precisely what I am talking about when I say God gives us proofs.

What Is Power?

When you think of power, what picture comes to mind? Sumo wrestlers? Offensive linemen (football players not foul-mouthed railroad or telephone line workers)? Weight lifters are also called power lifters. They all possess brute strength. And what about mental power—brain power? My husband, Gerry, comes to mind. He's always thinking. He wears me out with all his thinking. He's idea driven; I'm task driven. That's probably why he married me—so I can help him accomplish his big ideas. Another person that comes to mind is my friend Terry Osgoode, a brilliant lawyer, wonderful mom, smart shopper, and all-around amazing person. Her Facebook profile recently mentioned how thrilled she was that she got paid to think and write. Brainiac! (I'm not jealous...really. Okay, I am a little, but I'm repenting even as I type.)

From horsepower to political influence, from manmade energy to the storms in nature, there are endless manifestations of power. But what about God's power? What does that look like? Creating the cosmos by simply speaking it into existence bespeaks a power so magnificent our human minds can't begin to comprehend it. Sending water to flood the earth and then holding back the waters of the Red Sea and the Jordan River? Big stuff. Bringing down Jericho's walls, stilling storms, raising the dead? Unfathomable. Does God still manifest His power today? His power has been recorded so magnificently in history, but some Christians doubt that God still moves mountains in our lives today. They miss opportunities to experience His power because they barricade themselves so thoroughly behind every material security this world has to offer so they don't need Him to make it to Friday. They believe they've got it all under control themselves.

Power for the Next Yes

How many yeses do you suppose Noah had to say before he got that ark built, the animals loaded, and the goods stored? How many steps does it take to reach the summit of Everest? If you count the steps of preparing your physical body, saving the money, and amassing your alpine gear before you get off the plane in Katmandu and look for a Sherpa, it takes hundreds of thousands of small steps. Standing on top of the world, mountaineers feel a tremendous sense of power because they realize they are standing on a piece of earth only available to a select few. However, the power that got them to that zenith, at its most basic level, was taking the next step. If you are a climber or have seen films of hikers nearing a peak, you've experienced or heard ragged breathing and the painfully slow and deliberate acts of placing one foot in front of the other to inch forward. God's power, while mighty and vast beyond measure, is usually metered out in small steps—some painfully slow and difficult to take and some as easy as a colt's playful leap. How much power do we need to follow God? Just enough for the next yes.

The complexity that holds many people back from climbing Everest is what holds many believers back from following God. The mountain is too high. The cost is too great. The commitment is too large. The air is too thin. The gear is too heavy to carry. Getting into good enough shape is too difficult. Not everyone can climb mountains, but *everyone can follow God!* Even when He calls us to scale mountains higher than any we've ever scaled before, we know we can because He will help us do it.

God's Power to Forgive

Many years ago I met a woman who epitomized the picture of God's power to move mountains in the lives of His followers. Agnes had one daughter who was grown and married and had two children of her own. One day Agnes received the call every parent prays will never come. Her daughter was murdered by her husband. Then he turned the gun on himself, but he only succeeded in blowing away part of his face. He was still alive, and the doctors were fighting to save his life.

Agnes's first reaction after dropping the phone and struggling to catch her breath was to run outside her farm home and scream to the skies, "Why? Why? Why?" Her precious daughter gone. Her grandchildren forever scarred. She was overwhelmed with grief and bitterness toward the man who had destroyed so many lives with one gunshot. The days and weeks went by in a blur of saying goodbye to what was and embarking on a new life, one they never expected. Agnes and her husband, both in their sixties, adopted their grandkids.

Several months went by before Agnes had a chance to slow down and take stock of all that happened. She hadn't turned away from God, even right after the murder when her heart was so broken, Agnes had kept praying, her pleas of "Why?" changing to "What now?" And God had led her, one step at a time, through the maze of rearranging their lives. Although He hadn't instigated the murder, God responded by giving Agnes a new dream—to raise her grandkids in a godly, loving home.

Agnes also sensed that God was leading her to something even bigger than accepting the loss of her only daughter. Even bigger than raising her daughter's children. She sensed that God wanted to give her yet another dream: to know the freedom of complete forgiveness. He was asking her to forgive the murderer she'd once loved as a son.

"How can I do that, Lord?" she cried.

"Go see him," He answered. Nothing more. One *simple, immediate, possible* directive.

Her son-in-law had been quickly tried after recovering enough from his ghastly wound. He was convicted of second-degree murder and given a life sentence. The prison was only a few hours away from Agnes's home. Because Agnes had been following God one yes at a time for most of her adult life, she didn't hesitate to say yes, although it was hard. She would go see her former son-in-law. She knew she could go to the prison, walk in the door, and find the courage to face him. But she didn't know how she could possibly forgive him. Agnes had walked with God long enough to know that obedience was the only pathway to "abundant life."[7] She trusted that the God who put the ram in the thicket for Abraham would provide the power she needed at the very moment it was required.[8]

Agnes and her husband found daycare for their grandkids and drove to the prison, praying all the way for God to "show up in power." They arrived in the early afternoon, submitted themselves to the humiliating routine of getting through the layers of security, and were finally shown into a room sparsely furnished with a table and a few chairs. Agnes's heart was racing and her breath was coming in little gasps. Neither of them had seen their son-in-law since before the crime. She asked God for the strength to see the face of the man who had murdered her beloved daughter.

Holding It Together

Before she had a chance to compose herself, her son-in-law shuffled into the room. He had his head down, but she could see that he had a belt wrapped around his face. When he sat down across from them and raised his head she saw the shattered remains of what had once been a face she loved. The belt that tried to hold it together couldn't hold back the tears that streamed from his eyes that were clouded with sorrow.

"I forgive you," were the first words out of Agnes' mouth, even before she said hello. "I love you," was next. She meant it. She says God gave her the words and emotions. She can't explain how she could say them any other way.

Agnes told me years later, when we met and she shared her story, that God's power to forgive, absent for so many months, dropped into her heart the minute she saw her ex-son-in-law's pitiful face. She trusted God and said yes with her feet, and God released His power to love and forgive.

He's Still Parting Seas

God's power still parts seas, but if we don't say yes to the next step and start walking toward the shoreline, we'll never see it. And please don't think that God waits for us to get to the edge of the sea, wondering if and when we'll show up; He comes after us, gives us a picture-promise (dream), and then walks with us every step until we arrive at our destination. He was with Agnes as she took care of each little detail that was a small step between His request for her to make the prison visit and her arrival in that visitation room where His power to forgive swept through like a rushing wind.

Agnes continues to walk a difficult road. Her grandson, four years old at the time, bore the worst scars of the trauma. As a 16-year-old, he is filled with misery and hate. He struggles in school and has few friends. Agnes walks alongside him, loving him every step of the way, praying unceasingly for him, and modeling the joyful freedom that forgiveness brings. She told me she didn't know how she would be able to raise her grandkids if God hadn't freed her from bitterness and given her the power to forgive. She is trusting God to heal and restore her grandson's heart. Meanwhile her granddaughter, like her mother before her, brings joy and laughter into Agnes's life, and she is deeply grateful.

If you met Agnes today you would have no indication of the suffering she has endured, despite the toll it took. Her eyes are clear and her face is often wreathed in smiles because she has allowed God to free her from yesterday and give her the courage and hope for today and tomorrow.

We all face mountains at various points in our lives. Thankfully, very few face ones as steep and formidable as what Agnes has climbed with God's power. However, struggle is relative. The struggles you and I are in right now probably seems as monumental to us as Agnes' seemed to her. God's power is just as available to us as it was, and is, to her. He will give us dreams and then lead us, one yes at a time, to take all the steps needed to get to the shoreline where He will part the sea for us so we can cross over and be free. He will walk with us every step of the way as we make our way, sometimes with agonizing slowness, to the sea.

God's Power to Love

As a young teacher with only one year of experience teaching Grade 10 Language Arts, I was offered a job at a much larger school teaching Grade 11. Seventy people had applied for this job, but I got it. I was scared to death, but I knew without a shadow of doubt that this job was God's dream for me. When I took the job in the bigger school, I was barely 23 years old, a new bride, and the only female in an English department that up until my hire was comprised of six men, all of them seasoned veterans.

The Runaway Class

I walked into my first class feeling like a rodeo clown with a bum leg and a bull's-eye on my backside. It didn't help that it was already the third official day of classes. (I missed the first two days because I was recovering from ripping a layer of skin off my eyeballs when I removed the contact lenses that had adhered to my dry eyes at the end of a 16-hour day.) Weakened, sleep deprived by the pain, wearing dark glasses to shield my still-sensitive eyes from the light, pressured by the responsibility, and scared by my lack of experience, I made a rather faltering start. I failed to inspire the classes I taught that day to follow my leadership. I didn't know where *I* was going so it was pretty near impossible for them to follow me.

By the end of the first week I moved from scared to panic. Midway through the second week I was so daunted by this mountain I couldn't seem to climb that during my prep period I retreated to the English teacher's workroom to hide. In the workroom each of us had our own carrel. In an adjoining room was our private library and a large conference table. I barely made it inside the door, slumped into the nearest chair at the table, and dropped my head into my hands. It took all my effort to hold back tears. The room was empty so I closed my eyes and tried to pray, but no words came.

The door burst open and Maurice Stadnyk, a Grade 12 teacher, bustled in with an armload of books. He was midway through a class but had stepped out for a minute to drop off a large pile of books his students had returned to him.

"Well hello, Sister Mary Mercy!" he greeted me when he plunked down his load in the library and noticed me off to the side. All the men in the English department thought that since I was married to an ordained man of the cloth, I must be like a married nun, so I went by a new ecclesiastical name every day according to their whim. I took it as it was intended—good fun. I usually laughed at the more creative monikers. But today I wasn't laughing. He noticed immediately.

"Have I interrupted your matins?" he asked, his lips twitching at his own humor.

"Matins are morning prayers," I droned. "It's mid-afternoon."

"So what's up? You don't look too happy."

I sensed genuine concern in his voice. Maurice, besides being the most experienced teacher on staff, was also the most beloved by his students and was well respected by teachers and parents. Maurice had already published the first of the many books he would write. He'd asked me during the job interview what I was writing, and I was embarrassed to admit I wasn't writing anything.

The Root of the Problem

I was desperate and didn't know what to do so I swallowed my pride and admitted the truth. "I'm blowing it," I confessed. "I can't control the students. They're running away with my classes." My eyes began to leak despite my effort to avoid crying in front of my colleague. I wondered if he was mentally running through the list of 69 other candidates that had been interviewed and turned down for the job I had, by God's grace, managed to win. He was probably wishing they'd chosen one of them.

"I've only got a minute," Maurice said, looking right into my face. "Let me ask you one thing." He paused.

"Do you love them?"

Love them? How could I love them? They scared me to death. They felt more like enemies than friends. How do you love your enemies? I knew Jesus had done it and commanded us to do the same, but I knew I didn't have the power to accomplish it. As these thoughts whirled through my head, I was so choked up I didn't trust my voice. I simply shook my head giving Maurice the answer he already suspected.

"There's your problem," he said quietly with great kindness and generosity. He had been young once and probably scared too. He didn't judge. And with that he was out the door.

When Maurice walked out, I prayed one of my "little faith" prayers: "God, I don't have the power to love these kids. I don't know how I'm going to do it, but I need Your help." God hears our heart-cries, and He *always* answers, but not necessarily right away. God had given me a dream through Maurice's mouth: love my students. I didn't know how to achieve it or where to begin so, for a while, nothing changed. Nothing in me, that is. But trouble was brewing and about to boil over.

Take This Job and…Love It

A couple of weeks later the situation in my classroom was still unimproved. As I was getting ready for work one morning the phone rang. I picked it up and listened to an irate parent accusing me of being the reason her 18-year-old son was suddenly having nightmares. She informed me that she would be calling the principal's office next. My 20-minute commute to the school was spent wiping away tears and praying for strength. The only thing I had in my favor, I believed, was that I knew without a doubt this job was God's dream for me. I was on the right path. I was exactly where He wanted me to be—but I sure never expected this.

When I got to work I went straight to the principal's office to alert him to the incoming call. The mother had beat me to it. I was told that a meeting was set up for after school involving the student, his mother, the principal, the vice principals, the guidance counselor, and me. Fortunately, I felt support and understanding from my colleagues, who were probably waiting to get all the facts before deciding what to believe. The student in question was not in class that day, thankfully.

We gathered at four o'clock as planned and took seats around a large conference table. The mother and son were on my left, the principal and his cohorts on my right. I was seated between them, a perfect location for being drawn and quartered, I thought without humor. My stomach was in knots. The student's mother glared at me through red eyes and didn't return my shaky smile. I admired her for facing a roomful of people she probably expected would stand together or maybe even gang up on her.

The principal opened the meeting by explaining that we were all there to address a parental concern and then he invited the mother to take the floor. As she began to describe with high emotion the things she'd heard her son and his friends talk about when they gathered at her house after school to hang out, her son sank lower and lower in his seat. The teacher she was describing was a real witch all right. It just so happened she wasn't me. She wasn't anyone on our staff. She was the creation of a group of boys who hated English class. Some of them were even taking it a second time after having failed it the previous year. And everyone in the room knew it except the mom.

"Well, tell them. Tell them the things you told me!" she commanded, turning to her son.

He looked up at me, his cheeks aflame and his eyes brimming. He admitted in a whisper, "Not everything I said was true. We might have exaggerated a little."

Left Behind

I don't recall much of what happened during the rest of the meeting other than it was concluded that the reason this young man was having nightmares was because he was terrified of failing English for a second time, being teased, and getting left behind as his classmates graduated and moved on. Looking for someone to blame, he had picked me. And I can't really blame him. I was an easy target as I tried to stay one trick ahead of my unruly students. Both mother and son apologized and asked for forgiveness. I assured them of that and more. I offered to give the student individual help and support.

The next day the young man showed up early for class, asked to be moved to a seat near the front, and, swallowing his pride, raised his hand and asked a question for the first time during the lecture portion of the class. I was impressed...more than impressed. I was won over. I loved that kid! What courage. What humility. By God's grace the love I felt for that brave student opened my eyes to the wonderful qualities in the other students. I began to love them. And they sensed it. They responded to my love instead of reacting to my orders.

The atmosphere in all my classes improved day-by-day. Three tough guys in one of my classes who had made my life miserable in September were "bringing apples" by Thanksgiving. By Christmas they pooled their money to buy me bookends—beautiful, hand-carved wooden praying hands. I still have them 30 years and many moves later.

Follow Him to the Edge

What brought about the change? Undoubtedly it was love. But it was love I didn't have the power to generate on my own. God's power to love through me was released when I said yes to His dream to love my students. He brought me through the difficulty and pain one yes at a time. I had gone to the edge of the sea and His power parted the waters so my students and I could walk to the promised land and freedom on the other side.

Every morning during that painful season of failing to lead my students in love, what gave me the power to say yes to a job I hated and was failing miserably at was the assurance that I was on the right path. I was where God wanted me. And now I look back, glad that He took me through this time of trouble because I got to see His power conquer my sea of fear and lack of confidence as He led me to the freedom to love on the other side.

Walking in His Will

When God comes to us and shares His strength and power to help us overcome our barriers of fear or failure, He proves He is real and assures us we're on the right path. Knowing we are where God wants us to be makes it easier to keep moving forward when the water gets deep. Even though I was struggling and not living up to the potential my colleagues believed I had, I knew I was exactly where God wanted me to be. I also knew I wasn't doing such a hot job. That knowledge gave me power to say yes to God day after day. His strength gave me the will to keep going back into what felt like a den of lions rather than a classroom of students. Not only does God give us power in the moments when we need it most, but He also gives us the knowledge that we are walking in His will, which empowers us to keep working toward achieving our dreams.

If you aren't experiencing God's power in your life today, *don't go looking for His power.* What you do need to do is *look for Him.* Seek the Giver and ask Him to give you His dream and the means to achieve it. God will give you proofs, the chocolates on the trail, as you say yes when He calls.

If you're still not sure how to follow Him, here are some simple suggestions:

- Get a copy of *Experiencing God* by Henry Blackaby. Work through the first eight lessons to discover how you can know and do God's will. If you'd like help going through the chapters, I invite you to join a free, online study I teach at http://www.e-quip.net/presentations/show/2321. The seminar consists of 8 one-hour lessons.

- If you're involved in or know of a Bible-believing church, ask the pastor for guidance and resource suggestions. Ask the pastor to pray with you.

- If you know or are acquainted with other Christ-followers, ask them to point you to biblical resources and opportunities. Ask them to pray with you too.

[Jesus said,] "Keep asking, and it will be given to you. Keep searching and you will find. Keep knocking, and the door will be opened to you. For everyone who asks receives, and the one who searches finds, and to the one who knocks the door will be opened."⁹

Overcoming Barriers

God's willingness to release His power to help us overcome barriers is such a blessing. And He releases that power every time we say a *simple, immediate, possible* yes. And when we experience His power, we have proof that He is real, that we heard Him right, and that we are on the right path. The sure knowledge that we are living the dreams He gives us helps us continue to follow Him even when the going gets tough.

God's presence, God's peace, God's power—all are proofs He is real, He is alive, He still works miracles, and He wants to be personally involved in every aspect of our daily lives. These proofs are the manifestations of the invisible God we follow by faith. We sense His presence. We experience His peace. We hear Him. When we are swept along by His power to accomplish something that is beyond our human abilities, we see Him at work. All these events strengthen our faith muscle. And since we walk by faith, it never hurts to gain muscle to help us toward the "goal [of] the prize promised by God's heavenly call in Christ Jesus," as the apostle Paul put it.¹⁰ What is that prize? That goal? Paul said, "My goal is to know Him and the power of His resurrection."¹¹

If you focus on knowing God, the power will come. And it is by His power alone that we get what we need—another proof we followers with "little faith" rely on to fuel our journey.

PROVISION

~~~

Abraham named that place The Lord Will Provide,
so today it is said: "It will be provided on the Lord's mountain."

GENESIS 22:14

Ask any teenager who is waiting for the opportune moment to tell his parents he just hit a tree with their new car, and he'll tell you timing is everything. God is the master of perfect timing. He hears our cries and responds by providing what He knows we need (and that's not always what we ask for). He has an eternal viewpoint, while we usually are seeking immediate relief from our present circumstance. He has a wider scope to consider; we have tunnel vision. He wants to impact as many people as possible; we care mostly about our immediate circle of family and friends and us. When we look back and recognize God's provision and realize it had far greater impact than the action we were seeking, it can be a powerful proof that God is real, He cares, He wants to be involved in our personal lives, and He knows best.

Aron Ralston's story, as told in his New York Times bestseller *Between a Rock and a Hard Place* illustrates the principle of the importance of timing.[1] Ralston, a self-proclaimed risk-taker who has a passion for climbing, hiking, and skiing, tells the grisly story of his six-day ordeal trapped in a remote canyon in Utah.

Setting off on a solo hike of Horseshoe Canyon early one Saturday in May, Ralston parked his truck at the end of his planned 30-mile trek. Then he took his bicycle out of the truck bed and cycled back to where he would begin the hike. His plan was to hike to the truck and then drive back to the trailhead and pick up his bike on the way home.

About halfway into his hike down a deep narrow canyon, he encounters several chockstones. These are huge boulders the size of refrigerators wedged between the canyon walls. He ducks under the first two but the others have to be scaled. After climbing atop one of the stones he feels it begin to shift. As it rotates he knows he's in trouble so he lets himself fall nine feet to the canyon floor below. The stone falls toward him, hits and bounces off his left hand, and lodges between the narrow canyon walls a few feet above ground. His right hand is pinned between the boulder and the canyon wall.

As the minutes turn to hours, Ralston endures the agonizing pain of his injuries and deals with the awful knowledge that no one—not his family, friends, coworkers, or the Utah State Park staff knows where he is. The high-traffic hiking season is still weeks away, and his location means he is unlikely to be discovered by other hikers. His penchant for solo adventure has caught up with him as he realizes he's broken the cardinal rule by failing to log an itinerary with anyone prior to his trip.

He believes he'll probably die of thirst before anyone notices he's missing. And once he is reported missing, it could take days to locate his truck, which would only give a vague clue as to where he might be in the labyrinth of canyons he had chosen to explore. As reality sinks in, Ralston begins to understand that he must find a way to free himself because nobody is going to come along in time to help him survive.

A Hideous Reality

His first idea is to move the boulder. But he can't get it to budge. He hacks at the stone with his utility knife and a small rock until his already damaged left hand is almost unusable. After several hours with little measurable effect, he admits defeat and moves on to his second option: Since he can't move the rock, he'll have to remove his arm. His voice rises a few octaves as he speaks this hideous thought aloud. He already knows that his blunted knife blade can never saw through his arm bone so he's stuck, literally.

As he considers his predicament and looks for solutions over the next hours and days, he grows weaker and weaker. Raging thirst, exposure to cold nights, lack of sleep, and horrific pain take their toll. It isn't until the sixth day, still alive against all odds, that Ralston gets the idea that has eluded him until now: He doesn't have to cut through the bones. He can break the two forearm bones by using the viselike grip of his imprisonment as leverage. He wonders why he hasn't thought of this earlier since it seems ridiculously obvious now.

I will spare you the gory details of his on-the-spot surgical procedure that is told with chilling clarity in the book. Suffice to say, he frees himself, applies a tourniquet to his arm, and begins the long hike out of the canyon. Blood loss and exhaustion exact a price, and after several miles he is nearing the end of his resources. Suddenly he sees a family of hikers in the distance. He calls for help. The hikers had been advised to be on the lookout for a lost hiker because, by this time, Ralston's truck had been found and a search had been launched. One of the hikers runs for miles to get help, and the helicopter, pilot, and crew that were already part of the search for Ralston soon arrive to airlift him to a hospital.

Seeing the Miracle

Getting back to the timing of realizing he could break his forearm, Ralston shares why it took so long to solve the riddle of how to free himself:

> In recounting the story [to the men in the helicopter], I begin to wonder about the timing of the helicopter and how it found me in the canyon at the perfect moment when I needed it. If it had been an hour later, I would have died waiting for help. Or if I had figured out how to cut off my arm two days earlier...there wouldn't have been a helicopter, and I would have bled out before getting to my truck.[2]

When Ralston had prayed for a miracle on Day 3 of his entrapment, he wanted to see God break the rock that was pinning him into two pieces so it would fall to the ground and release him. That didn't happen. God was silent. By his own admission Ralston was not a serious

God-follower, so he decides to ask the devil if he would like to help him out. He gets no response from him either.

What Ralston later realizes was that the miracle God provided wasn't to shatter the rock that held him. No, it was to blind him to the solution long enough to allow his rescuers to be in place to save his life. Ralston sums it up this way:

> For all that has happened and the opportunities still developing in my life, I feel blessed. I was part of a miracle that has touched a great number of people in the world and I wouldn't trade that for anything, not even to have my hand back.[3]

Lord Help Me, Not Now—But Right Now!

Ralston's request for a miracle and his expectation of how that would look is how many of us think when we ask God to provide for our needs:

- "Lord, I'm facing financial ruin. Drop a gold brick from heaven. Make that two gold bricks."

- "God if I don't quit smoking I will die. Take away my addiction to nicotine. And please make my lungs pink by Thursday—I have a doctor's appointment."

- "Father, I need to lose 50 pounds by Friday. It's my 10-year high school reunion. Remove these extra hips!"

When we pray for a miracle, when we seek God's *provision,* it can be something as small as wanting relief from a cold to asking for healing from cancer. It can be as little as asking for heavenly help to raise money for a mission trip to asking God to intervene so you don't lose your million-dollar business. It can be a request to protect your teens on their road trip or a broken-hearted plea to free your adult child from a severe addiction. As we pray, we are sometimes so busy scanning the horizon for divine liposuction that we can be momentarily blinded, as Aron Ralston was, to the wider scope of God's viewpoint. We are so focused on our own situation and our own assessment of what we think we need to get us out of this momentary jam that we forget that almighty God is involved. He always has a far bigger dream for us than we would dream up on our own.

God's Bigger Dreams

The story of redemption through forgiveness is told in Tom Elliff's book *The Red Feather*. Tom's father, a long-time pastor and Tom's hero, shocked his grown kids, his wife, and everyone who knew him the day he announced he was leaving his marriage and his ministry.

I'm sure Tom's mother, Jewell, and all who loved her, prayed that her husband would come to his senses, return to her, resume his ministry, and life would go back to normal. That was a good prayer, a worthwhile prayer. I have prayed many prayers just like that. However, God had a broader goal in mind. His plans included a provision that would include suffering but also extend healing and hope beyond the small world of one family's broken hearts.

Not long after her husband left, Jewell began to show symptoms of confusion and was diagnosed with Alzheimer's. She quickly slipped deeper and deeper into dementia as her adult children did everything they could to preserve her dignity and provide for her safety. The final blow was a brain aneurism that should have taken her life in a matter of hours—days at most. But Jewell hung on for five weeks, in a coma for all but a tiny fraction of time. She kept repeating two words three times each: "Want! Want! Want!" and "Forgive! Forgive! Forgive!"[4]

The miracle of forgiveness she was looking for took place in Jewell's hospital room. Shortly after her children figured out their mother was trying to say she wanted to extend forgiveness—a forgiveness she'd already modeled by her frequent prayers for both her ex-husband and his second wife—the phone rang. It was the man she longed to forgive. Even though he had not been in touch with his family for three years, he'd heard of his first wife's illness. Not realizing its extent, he'd called hoping to speak to her.

Tom, Jewell's son, answered the phone. He explained the situation including that Jewell was in a coma. When Tom heard what his dad wanted to say, he agreed to place the receiver by Jewell's ear so she could hear (if she still could hear and understand) what he had to say. Tears flowed down his mother's face after Tom put the phone by her ear and she heard the precious words she'd longed to hear. Miraculously, she was able to murmur her forgiveness in response to her former husband's confession and request.

Within days Tom's dad flew in, and the entire family experienced the joy of forgiveness and reconciliation as they gathered around the bedside of the woman who so courageously modeled Christ's love and forgiveness.

Standing near her casket not many days later, Tom writes, "Our mother, bruised by a sad separation and stricken as she was with Alzheimer's, was not going down in defeat but in glorious triumph. In some ways, Mother's last days were perhaps her greatest days."[5]

Does God provide? Yes. Does His provision meet our expectations? Not always. Sometimes God has bigger dreams. Dreams that reach far beyond our little circle of influence to touch the world and bring healing and hope to more than just those near and dear to us. God used Jewell's "long, loving arms that seemed able to wrap totally around you" to wrap a hurting world in it's far-reaching embrace.[6] Jewell's life stands as proof that God provides and His provision can bring reconciliation to a broken family and provide a redemptive story of hope to millions.

Cesar's Story

You may not have heard of Cesar Parra yet, but you probably will. His passion for telling people about Jesus takes him all over the world to share a simple method he calls "Action 52."[7]

Cesar was born in Chile and immigrated to Canada via Argentina with his parents and sister when he was 8 years old. His parents had a dream: They wanted to provide their kids with opportunities they never had and give them a better future. They moved into a tiny apartment in the worst area of Toronto. Cesar's dad worked hard, and before long they were thrilled to check off the first item on their wish list: a brand-new car. Things were looking up.

Cesar fantasized about all the stuff he might get for Christmas now that his family had more disposable income, and his excitement grew daily. Cesar loved soccer so maybe his dad would buy him new soccer equipment. But before Christmas came, Cesar's dad separated from his wife and family by moving out. Cesar's brave new world collapsed. He was incredulous. Being abandoned filled him with a rage that threatened to consume him.

The first time he saw his dad after that was on a cold winter day as he and his mom and sister were hurrying across an icy parking lot at the mall, hoping to catch the approaching bus so they wouldn't have to wait for the next bus while shivering in the cold and loaded with packages. Suddenly a familiar, shiny new car glided by. The driver saw them and quickly looked away, but not before Cesar got a real good look at the couple inside the car, snug and warm. It was his dad and his girlfriend.

Rage

Cesar exploded. He yelled at his mother, expressing his pent-up anger that his dad, their dream car, their dream life, had been stolen from them. At that moment he hated his dad, and he really hated the woman who had tricked him into leaving them. His mother, Maria, stopped in her tracks, forcibly sat him down on a raised curb, and got right in his face. What she said in rapid-fire Spanish Cesar will never forget. "Your dad loves you," she said. "And even though he's gone a little crazy right now, and you can't understand what he's doing, don't ever doubt that he loves you. No matter what he does, he is still your father and you need to love him."

One Simple, Immediate, Possible Yes

Not long after Cesar's dad left, he and his girlfriend had a baby boy. Cesar was further enraged. First he was abandoned, now he was "replaced." He told his mother he hated the new baby. Once again Maria gave it to him straight: "Tony is your new brother. He's family. You will go visit him." Cesar's mom intuitively understood that she couldn't make Cesar forgive his father or love his new brother, so she asked him to do one, simple, immediate, possible thing—go to see them. She hoped that visit-by-visit Cesar would discover how to love and forgive as she had. And that's exactly what happened.

While Tony was still a toddler, his birth mother abandoned the baby and Cesar's dad. Because Cesar's dad couldn't afford extended child-care, Maria took over more and more of Tony's care. Before Tony was six, she offered to take him in fulltime, and he became Cesar's little side-kick. Cesar's father never moved back with his family. He married again, but he stayed involved in the lives of his kids, especially their education. When Tony's mother returned to Toronto a decade later, Maria made sure that Tony reconnected with her, teaching him the same message of love and forgiveness she'd given Cesar years earlier. After spending weekends with her for a year, at the age of 15 Tony decided his mom needed someone to take care of her, so he went to live with her.

A New Creation

By this time Cesar was 25 years old, working a dead-end job, play-ing soccer for five Toronto teams, partying in Latino clubs most nights, running with a bunch of tough guys, and being angry all the time. His dream of being discovered and playing pro soccer had never material-ized. He had a reputation on the field and in the streets for getting even in the most brutal ways. If anyone dared to trip him, throw an elbow, or give him a cheap shot, Cesar made sure to repay double what he got.

When Maria started attending a Spanish-speaking church she invited him repeatedly to come. She knew she couldn't make Cesar love God or change his lifestyle, but she could ask him to say yes to one simple, immediate, possible thing—go to church with her. He even-tually gave in and went. Once. After visiting the church, some of the young people called Cesar and asked if they could visit. One of them was a raven-haired beauty that Cesar had spotted in the choir at church. He had asked his mother about her when they got home. Maria let him have it straight: "That's Mary. She is the pastor's daughter, and she is a *very* good girl. Don't you touch her. I'll take the broom to you if you even look at her!" His mother was a saint, but she wasn't stupid. Cesar says they went through a lot of brooms over the years.

Mary was one of the three teens who came to visit Cesar at home.

Mary told Cesar the simple truth about Jesus: "He loves you; He died in your place to pay for your sins; He wants to come in to your life. Will you let Him in?" Cesar had never heard such good news: Forgiveness for all the bad things he'd done? Hope for a better future? All he had to do was say yes? Cesar invited Jesus into his life immediately.

Will It Last?

Even though he felt different, like something had happened to him when he asked Jesus in, Cesar didn't think it would last. Nothing ever had. But the next day, on the soccer field, a strange thing happened. A player on the opposing team, a new guy who obviously didn't know Cesar's reputation, tripped him and then, for good measure, kicked him in the ribs. Everybody froze. Neither team wanted to miss the beating Cesar would deliver once he got back on his feet.

Jumping up and facing his attacker Cesar balled his fists but before he could take a swing, something stopped him. *God loves you and gave His Son to die for you*, he remembered. *You are a new creation.* His hands relaxed. He shook his head and told his opponent who was crouching, ready to defend himself, "Iss okay, man. Fogedaboudid. Less play." He ran back to his position. Shockwaves rippled across the field. Cesar's first Christ-like act generated so much buzz that he eventually introduced almost every player on his team to Jesus. Nobody had told Cesar not to fight; it was the voice of the Holy Spirit he heard and said yes to. He was beginning to grow in the simple way God designed—one simple, immediate, possible yes at a time.

The Tribute

Cesar's dad was the first person he led to Christ. Then his dad's wife. Then eventually Tony. And scores more. Cesar's mom never remarried; she kept her factory job until she retired. "She's okay. She's happy," Cesar says. At Tony's big Italian wedding last year, when it was time for toasts and tributes, his Italian mom was called upon to say a few words. She took the microphone and said, "I should not be standing here today. Someone else deserves to be in this place of honor. Many years ago, I did a foolish thing. I set my eyes on a man and determined to get him any way I could. And I did. That man was Tony's father. I was young and foolish, and before long I abandoned both of them. Tony's dad had a hard time caring for him so his ex-wife took Tony in and raised him." Pointing to where Cesar's mom was seated, her voice broke when she said, "*She* is his *real* mother. I want to pay tribute to Maria today." That day, at the wedding, Cesar introduced several of Tony's relatives to Jesus.

Even when her world was shattered, her heart broken, her dreams unfulfilled, Maria was able to live with dignity and integrity, focusing on what she still had, not on what she'd lost. She found happiness by spending time in God's presence, by living in His peace, by relying on His power to forgive and to love, and by trusting in God's provision. She modeled God's love, forgiveness, and grace for Cesar and Tony and many others. Maria, an unassuming little woman who worked on an assembly line in a factory for decades and barely speaks English, is a spiritual giant whose influence will span continents and generations.

I met Maria recently at a conference in Toronto. Cesar was there, speaking and playing the congas in a Latino worship band. Having heard about her for years, I couldn't wait to give her a hug and tell her what a hero and role model she was for thousands of people who heard her son speak. Not tall myself, I towered over this diminutive little woman with grandchildren clustered around her. I leaned down so we could embrace. I told her what a spiritual giant I thought she was, and her response revealed her humble heart: "My English is not so good. I hope you are not disappointed to meet the real person behind Cesar's stories."

God's Ways Are Not Ours

Sometimes we don't understand what God is doing. The Bible tells us God's ways are not our ways nor are our thoughts like His.[8] But the Bible also says in dozens of places and many ways that God loves us with an everlasting love. And He continues to extend His faithful love to us.[9] There are times many of us feel like Cesar did—except about God. Cesar felt like an angry, abandoned immigrant boy when he watched his father glide by snug and warm and sharing his love with someone else. We hear about God's love and amazing provision for others, and we wonder why we're left out in the cold:

- If God is love, why did He allow our little boy—our only child—to chase his ball into the street and get struck down and killed by a car?

- If God is love why did He let us lose our ranch? It was our heritage for four generations and our only savings for the future.

- If God is love why would He allow my business partner to lose my entire savings earned from 30 years of hard work when I left him in charge to attend seminary?

- Having a family is all I've ever wanted. If God is love why won't He help me get pregnant?

- If God is love and He wants people to know Him, why would He allow our pastor, the best evangelist I've ever known, to get Lou Gehrig's disease (ALS), lose his ability to speak, and quickly die?

How do we reconcile a loving God with a hurting world? How can we say God provides when so many people suffer such great losses? We can do it one story at a time, beginning with the Greatest Story ever told: "God *proves* His own love for us in that while we were still sinners Christ died for us!"[10] Jewell Elliff *proved* God's love by drawing on God's power to pray for her ex-husband and his new wife and to forgive her ex-husband for abandoning her. Cesar's mom, Maria, proved God's love by teaching forgiveness and love to her children, by raising Tony as her own, and by forgiving her ex-husband. God's provision for these godly women gave them what they needed to overcome the barriers that threatened to hold them back from following God wholeheartedly in faith and joy.

Everyone suffers losses, from children dying to foreclosures on homes, from losing savings to infertility. Every person has his or her stories. Some tell of God's timely provision. Some tell of the broad scope of God's provision. But sometimes we don't know or understand what God is doing. The couple who lost their only child were able to have two more even though they were nearing the end of their child-bearing years. However, they couldn't reconcile their loss with a loving God, so their pain has become a barrier between God and them.

Some of the others never regained their losses. No babies came, the ranch was gone forever, the savings were not recouped, and the pastor died. But every one of them recognized God's provision to help them carry on. And they saw how God provided during the struggles. A van equipped for a handicapped driver was given to the pastor with ALS right when he needed it. The childless couple saw how God arranged for their arms of love to embrace the children of relatives and friends, sometimes for years at a time, even though they never had children of their own.

God's Presence, Peace, Power, and Provision

God gives each of us His dreams. Some God-given dreams have dark valleys in them, but all His dreams will bring us into His presence where we find peace, power, and His miraculous provision when we follow them one yes at a time. And one of the biggest miracles is that He wants to use *our stories* as proof to others that He is real, He is alive, He cares, He wants to be personally involved in our lives, and He wants to use us to change and bring hope to the world we live in. Say yes to His dream for you and expectantly watch for His guidance and provision.

10

PRESENCE

⬥

God gives His Spirit not to those who long for Him,
not to those who pray for Him,
not to those who desire to be filled always, but
He does give His Holy Spirit to them that obey Him.[1]

HUDSON TAYLOR

When my husband, Gerry, was 14, his parents drove from Southern Saskatchewan to Montreal, Quebec, a four-day journey, to attend Expo 1967. They left their youngest son with an auntie back home, but took their four other boys, ranging in age from 6 to 14, and brought along an older cousin, Monique, to help keep the boys entertained en route.

Monique, at 16, was a genius when it came to keeping active boys mentally engaged on a long drive. She had an endless fund of travel games in her repertoire, but her best scheme of all was the way she kept the boys busy while their parents cooked supper every night in various campgrounds. After the boys had set up their tent, hung their clothesline, and unloaded the car, Monique would holler: "Snipe hunt!" and off they'd go. Monique had told them on the first stop of the trip that she would award a substantial cash prize to the boy who could find and catch a snipe on their journey. But snipes are elusive and scarce, she warned. They might have to look in several provinces before they spotted one.

"What does a snipe look like?" the eager boys asked.

"Oh you'll recognize it right away," Monique replied.

"What does a snipe do?" the curious boys wondered.

"All snipes do the same thing," Monique said with great seriousness.

"Where do snipes live?" the future hunters pleaded, hoping for clues.

"They're terrified of people—especially rambunctious boys—so they hide out in the snipiest places," she said. "You'd better get going," she urged. "But don't be noisy or you'll scare them away. Snipes come out to feed at dusk, and the sun is already going down!"

The boys scattered like a herd of spooked caribou. They combed the prairie grasslands of Saskatchewan and Manitoba. They tiptoed over the rocks of the Canadian Shield in Northern Ontario. They scoured the orchards of Southern Ontario and skulked along the riverbanks of Quebec. No snipes were spotted or captured, and Monique hung on to her money. The boys didn't figure out that the snipe hunt was a wild goose chase until halfway back on the way home. Monique wasn't as popular then as she had been on the way to the expo once the boys realized they'd been had.

The Elusive God

I hear from people all the time whose life journeys with God seem to resemble snipe hunts. Taryn read my first book *From Faking It to Finding Grace* and emailed me from South Africa:

> My own wilderness experience, which I am still going through, started about two years ago. I was praying one night for God to reveal Himself to me, because it felt like He was far from me and had been for a long time. I had just gone through about a month of fasting [from] TV. I was praying and being committed to Bible study. I felt I'd been doing everything right to find God. My heart's cry was to get to know Him on a much more intimate level (basically to fall in love with Him).

> I got so frustrated though, because even though I had been going through all the motions, I felt nothing. God seemed further away than ever! I realized that night that I was sick of living a mediocre Christian life. I felt I had lost God somewhere along the way.

So instead of drawing closer to God in this time, I retreated from Him. I told Him I was tired of doing all the right things in my walk with Him—serving and worshiping and reading my Bible—without the results I felt I needed: intimacy with God! I read passages from the Bible and felt like I was reading a boring book. I prayed and felt like I was talking to myself so I eventually grew bored. I worshiped but I didn't feel the old familiar warmth of the Holy Spirit. So I gave up on the devotional time and didn't open my Bible or pray for months and months.

Do Something!

I shared how I was feeling with my Bible-study group and friends. Their reactions and suggestions, although given in love, were "Do something about it!" I would hear the occasional "tut tut" when I told them I was still in a dry patch after 18 months. Their advice was to keep trying, keep reading the Bible, and keep praying. That it was up to *me* to change my life. I felt very misunderstood and very confused.

So that's why your book meant so much to me. To open it and read the echoes of my own heart—that God *will* pursue me, that there is nothing I can do to bring God back, that God loves me with an undying love, that God is walking through this wilderness with me. I felt like a huge burden was taken off my shoulders! To read that other people had gone through what I am told me I was on the right track. What a huge encouragement.[2]

Taryn and I corresponded a few times. Here's the last note I received from her:

I just wanted to share with you that I am well and truly out of the wilderness! God did amazing things to and through me over these past six months, and I have grown so much. I realized His love for me, and He drew so close to me. I look back at my time in the wilderness with a positive eye—without it I don't think I would have learned the lessons God was teaching me. Thanks again for your book that was instrumental in opening my eyes to what God was doing in my life.[3]

Sarah B. went looking for help for spiritual dryness in a bookstore and picked up *From Faking It to Finding Grace*. After reading the first two chapters she emailed me:

> I'm completely faking it right now. I grew up in a Christian home and went to Christian schools until college, and was very involved in Christian groups and activities. I'm not having doubts about what I believe—I'm just *missing a personal, passionate relationship with God* right now…I still go to church and am involved in a few areas. Though I'm not living a sinful lifestyle, I am so dry.

Sarah has lost her ability to sense God's presence. She wants to find God but doesn't know where He is. Like Taryn, she feels like she's on a snipe hunt for her elusive God.

Liz sent me this email: "I believe and have faith that God can move mountains. He is just not doing that for me. He is *real for other people, just not me*." Liz doesn't sense God's palpable presence. She is surrounded by people who are experiencing the peace, the power, and the provision that God's presence brings, but for her, God is as elusive as a snipe.

We Long for His Presence

Like the chosen priests of Old Testament times, believers today want to meet God. Like the Israelites as they journeyed from bondage in Egypt to freedom in Canaan, we want to follow God's cloud by day and God's fire by night so we know He is near. We want to sit at Jesus' feet like Martha's sister, Mary, did and soak up His teaching. We want to *experience* God. We want to see Him, hear Him, sense His presence. We want to know Him as more than just a casual acquaintance. We long for intimacy and a deep, personal connection with Him. But many believers go through seasons of dryness when it seems like God is hiding or maybe He's gone on vacation.

He Wants to Hang Out with Us

Here's some good news! It's true we want to know the living God intimately. And guess what? God wants to encounter us that way too! In the foreword to Brennan Manning's book *The Relentless Tenderness of Jesus,*[4] Dr. Larry Crabb wrote about a memorable encounter with Brennan Manning that impacted him in an unforgettable way. The two men were enjoying a quiet hour of relaxing, having both completed speaking at a convention for pastors. Soon they would leave for the airport and fly to their homes or on to other speaking engagements. Dr. Crabb asked Manning, "Where to next?" Manning replied that he was starting a seven-day silent retreat the following day. He was not leading it but taking it. Crabb's next question was exactly what I would have asked had I been sitting on that ninth floor hotel room balcony: "Brennan, help me here. I know you're into that sort of thing. How are you different after getting away for a week with just you and the Lord?"[5] He was basically asking, "What's in it for you, Brennan? What do you hope to get out of this? How will this make you a better writer, speaker, leader, husband, neighbor, church member, person?"

"I don't know what it does for me. I've never thought much about that. I just figure God likes it when I show up," Manning replied.[6]

Does his reply hit you between the eyes like it did me? Why do we find it so amazing that our great big, loving God would like it if we showed up? When God spoke audibly at Jesus' baptism saying, "You are My beloved Son. I take delight in You!" He was speaking to all His children who follow Him in faith.[7] Do you follow Him in faith? (Note: I said "in faith," not in perfection.) God takes delight in you. Every time you say yes to Him, He is especially pleased. All you have to do is "show up"!

It makes sense that God wants to spend time with us because that's why He created us. And He wouldn't come looking for us every time we wander off unless He truly loves us. Have you read the three stories in Luke, chapter 15? The parables about the lost sheep, the lost coin, and the lost son? The common theme in every one is that when we get lost (coin), or wander off (sheep), or run as far away as we can get from the Father who loves us (son), God pursues us with His undying love and calls us back to His heart. He wants more than to just *be involved in* our lives. He wants to *be* our lives. Charles Trumbull wrote in *The Life That Wins:*

> I had always known that Christ was my Saviour; but I had looked upon Him as an external Saviour, one who did a saving work *for* me from the outside, as it were; one who was ready to come alongside and stay by me, helping me in all that I needed, giving me power and strength and salvation. But now I knew something better than that. At last I realized that Jesus Christ was actually and literally within me...Was this not better than having Him as a helper, or even than having Him as an external Saviour: to have Him, Jesus Christ, God the Son, as my very own life?...Do you wonder that Paul could say with tingling joy and exultation, "To me to live is Christ"?[8]

God wants us to follow Him so closely that we will hear every whispered direction. Unfortunately, our ears are often clogged by our own agendas.

Don't Bug Me

Dwayne Bartley was a relatively new pastor of a quickly growing church in rural Alberta when, to his surprise and honor, he was invited to speak at an evangelism conference in Alaska alongside some "heavy hitters" in today's evangelical world. The topic he was given was "How to Share Christ in Any Given Situation." It was perfect, he thought. He had a lot to say on that topic since his specialty was telling people about Jesus. That's what made him want to get up in the morning. Spreading the Good News was the driving passion of his life. Many of the people he talked to about faith in Christ left the encounter as brand-new believers.

Because Dwayne had been invited at the last moment to pinch hit for a speaker who had become ill, he didn't have a lot of time to put his thoughts on paper. Since he had to fly from Calgary to Seattle to Anchorage, that gave him approximately five hours to organize his thoughts, put together an outline, and write out what he would say. He was looking forward to several hours of uninterrupted work.

When he boarded the plane in Seattle, Dwayne found his aisle seat, stowed his carry-on, and sat down with his Bible, a large legal pad, and a pen. He waited to fasten his seatbelt, knowing he would have to get up and let the passengers in the seats next to him get by. Silently he prayed that God would keep the seats empty or, hopefully, send people who would sleep or read or crochet or watch movies—anything but talk. Before long he saw a man coming down the aisle toward him. "He just looked like a talker. He was smiling. He sat more on me than beside me. He immediately began talking," Dwayne said.

Here's Yer Sign

"So, you goin' to Anchorage?"

Dwayne fought the urge to give a sarcastic comeback about being on a plane headed for Anchorage, along with everyone else. He was obviously going to Anchorage! The man talked and talked and talked, and between giving the shortest answers possible, Dwayne prayed that he'd shut up so he could work on his message about sharing Christ in any situation. "So what do you do?" the fellow finally asked after he had exhausted a wide range of topics and eaten up most of the flying time.

Typically Dwayne would answer the "What do you do?" question with something vague like "I sell life insurance," and then he would explain that the way to be sure of eternal life was through a relationship with Jesus. But this time, he wasn't trying to *make* conversation, he was trying to *kill* it. "I'm a Baptist preacher!" Dwayne replied.

"Do you know what I do?" Dwayne's seatmate asked. At that point Dwayne didn't care what the man did. He was worried about trying to impress a bunch of people at a conference in Alaska with his knowledge of how to share Christ. And his only chance to prepare his material was slipping away. "I do a similar job," the man declared. "I'm a trouble-shooter." Dwayne was completely baffled as to the similarity between being a Baptist preacher and a troubleshooter so, even though he didn't want to keep talking, he had to ask the man to explain. "Where we're alike is that some people don't even know they have a problem," the affable fellow explained with a big grin.

Ding!

With those words, Dwayne woke up to the truth of what was really going on. He had completely ignored the opportunity to talk to this man about a sin problem he probably didn't know he had. At that moment Dwayne realized he had really blown it. He had wasted five hours. He was almost out of time. He called out to God for forgiveness and help just as the plane taxied up to the gate.

Flustered and disappointed in himself, Dwayne stood, accidentally upending his briefcase all over the seats and aisle. As he bent to pick up his papers, he distinctly heard God whisper two words in his ear: "Follow Me." Dwayne's seatmate picked up a handful of gospel tracts that had tumbled onto the empty seat. They were titled "How Can You Have Eternal Life?" Reading the title, the man said he'd like to know the answer to that question. As the plane began to empty, Dwayne walked alongside his new friend, reading and explaining the good news about life in Christ. Before they got to the baggage carousel they both knelt in the airport hallway as people flowed around them. Dwayne led as the man prayerfully asked for his sins to be forgiven and for Jesus to come into his life.

Common Ground

You don't have to wonder what story Dwayne told when he gave his talk the next day at the evangelism conference. Dwayne says:

> I usually try to find some common ground when I share the gospel with someone, but here, I did nothing but try to get him to be quiet so I could do my work. When we prayed together in that airport, that was the ultimate experience of "follow Me." Evangelism is not trying to figure out who you will *do it to,* it's about *following Him.*[9]

What woke Dwayne up to the opportunity he almost missed? God's presence. God is real and He wants to speak to us. He led Dwayne to do something *simple, immediate,* and *possible:* Read the tract the interested man was already holding in his hand! Dwayne said yes to God, and because he did, another person stepped into an everlasting relationship with Jesus that day.

The barriers that almost succeeded in holding Dwayne back from following God were comparison and fear. As Dwayne thought about all the other speakers at the upcoming event, he felt intimidated. He wasn't in their league. His competitive drive pushed him to want to come up with a talk that would really impress the listeners as well as his fellow speakers. His fear was that he would get to Alaska, run out of time, and not be ready to speak when called upon. As a result, even though God had a dream for Dwayne—tell your seatmate about Me—Dwayne almost missed it. But God is a pursuing God, and He found a way to grab Dwayne's attention in the nick of time. Cool, isn't it!

Leaving the Wilderness

Would you like to know an amazing truth about the way God gave me back a sense of His presence that I'd lost during my years in the wilderness? I had to *say yes* to His dream for me and *step out* in faith *before* I could hear Him *within* my soul on a regular basis.

In the first few years of following Him one yes at a time out of wilderness, He seemed nearest when I was actively pursuing my dream to be a speaker for Christ. As I went, yes-by-yes, I came upon some chocolates on the trail (proofs) that told me I was on the right track. It took me a while to grow accustomed to the sound of His voice again so I could experience His nearness on a regular basis in my everyday life. Why do I call this amazing? Because to find *inner* connection, I had to make *outer* connections. To experience God's palpable presence, I had to say yes with my feet and go after the dream He gave me.

People in wilderness have stopped saying yes to God. I believe that often it's more the result of reacting in fear to their current suffering than it is stubborn rebellion, but it can be both. In my case, I had parked myself in my comfort zone, built up some impregnable walls to protect me from divine surprises (His dreams), and tried to live a life I could control. I no longer listened to His directives. As a matter of fact, I did everything I could to keep from hearing Him. Eventually I lost my ability to hear Him altogether as I drifted further and further into dryness.

Before I could experience His presence once again, I had to become reacquainted with the sound of His voice. The way He got me to listen for His voice again was to get me to follow His dream—to do things I couldn't do without Him. In other words, following His dream to bring hope to other "drifters" created a great need in me for the inner peace, power, and provision He offers. Every time He responded to my heart cry with one of His proofs, I experienced comfort and assurance that words can't really express. But my greatest reward for following God one yes at a time is that He has given me the priceless gift of a strong sense of His presence.

Yes, We're Human…

As Christians, we all want to know God and follow Him closely. We actively listen and earnestly seek Him. He, meanwhile, is also pursuing us to give us His dreams for our lives. Once we say yes to His dream, He leads us, one simple, immediate, possible yes at a time in the direction He wants to take us. We walk together because we are united in His Spirit. As we follow Him, He sends proofs of His presence, peace, power and provision. These proofs are like chocolates on the trail to remind us and convince us we're on the right path, God is real and alive, and we aren't walking alone. Sounds like a sweet deal, eh?

So why don't we all just follow Him and live happily ever after? The most obvious answer is because we're human. And as humans we have a tendency to collect a lot of baggage as we travel through life. Much of the stuff we add to our lives impedes our progress instead of enhancing it. Instead of building *ramps,* we build *walls.* The number and type of barriers are endless because everyone fights his or her own giants. Some common foes we face include fear, guilt, shame, comparison, pride, and doubt. These blockades hem us in, hold us back, and hinder our progress. We're going to explore how following God one yes at a time can turn barriers into ramps that take us from bondage to freedom and growth in Christ.

PART 3

BARRIERS

11

FEAR

The angel of the LORD encamps around those
who fear Him, and rescues them.

PSALM 34:7

After a supper of bologna and fried potatoes, the only way to stretch a small budget around a big family, my younger sister, Lisa, and I were told to go our parents' bedroom as soon as we finished doing the dishes. We were instantly nervous. Personal attention from our busy mom that didn't involve being fitted for an outfit she was sewing didn't usually work in our favor. We slowly finished up our evening chore without the usual ribbing and jostling and competing, both of us replaying in our minds all the possible sins we may have committed that somehow had been discovered. We rehearsed alibis and made up excuses as we wiped the plates.

Mom was perched on the edge of her bed, waiting for us when we sidled in, keeping our backsides well out of reach in case she had plans to mete out some swift justice. The room was small, like all the rooms in this tiny house—a house that had grown, room by room, but could never keep up as our family had grown. The seven girls shared two rooms and four beds while our only brother was allowed his own private cubicle in half of the closed-in porch Dad had added when Jim was around 10. We didn't sit on mom's bed, and we weren't invited to. We leaned against the wall, just over an arm's length away.

We were both so skittish it took us a while to recognize that Mom seemed more jumpy than we were. She appeared to be having a hard time finding the right words as she fumbled around, starting and stopping several times. However, we didn't let down our guard just in case this was the preliminary to her request for a full confession to our latest crime. In our small house in Northern Saskatchewan where six months of winter kept us indoors for long periods, there was always some sin we could be rightfully accused of as we tried and failed to get along with our boisterous siblings.

Baffled

In our nine- and eight-year-old brains, the muddled truth of what our mom was trying to explain was slow to seep in. It seemed like she was trying to warn us that some time soon we would start to bleed. Bleed? We were horrified! We had been spanked on several occasions, but never hard enough to cause a bruise—and now we were going to bleed? We flattened our bodies against the wall, as if someone were measuring our growth with a ruler and a pencil. We were too scared to ask "When?" since it might be imminent. I finally asked where this blood would come from, planning to protect that part of my body from her grasp.

"In this general area," Mom replied, looking down and making a circular motion with her right hand over her lap. I felt faint. That was a large area.

"Well, what about Jimmy?" I asked, wondering why he wasn't involved in this inquisition. Any uprising in the family big enough to lead to blood usually had him in the middle of it. That's when Mom realized how confused we were and that she was going to have to simplify things drastically before we would catch the drift of what she was trying to convey.

"No, this is only for girls," Mom explained, looking right at us for the first time. She most likely decided that since she was telling us about something we later—much later—came to understand was menses, she might as well throw in a little moral teaching as well. Her next comments were so vague and we were so innocent, I didn't figure it out until somewhere in my mid thirties. "You need to know it is a sin to touch yourself." She paused, unable to continue speaking. She simply circled her hand above her lap again.

We were completely baffled. How would we manage to clean ourselves after using the bathroom? We asked and were assured that toilet paper was still allowed as well as a soapy washcloth on bath night. "What about if we're itchy?" we asked in unison. As you can well imagine, any child who only gets a bath once a week and lives where mosquitoes were as thick as London fog during our brief summers, scratches often. Suddenly we worried that if a mosquito bit us through our thin little shorts on our bony little behinds we would be sinning every time we scratched the spot. Life was suddenly very complicated!

Mom sighed, grew agitated, shook her head rapidly a few times, and simply said, "That's all. You can go now."

Unknown Terrors

My sister and I skittered out of there as fast as our little legs could carry us. We quickly went through our nighttime routine of brushing our teeth, putting on our homemade pajamas, and crawling into the bed we shared. We both were awake for a long time, unable to talk about what was scaring us out of our wits—our mother's attempt to communicate something that we still weren't sure what she was talking about. We cried soundlessly, wiping our tears on the sheets in the dark, wondering when and where this bleeding would start. We were very careful to keep our hands on top of the blankets so we wouldn't unwittingly brush against our lap area and commit a sin.

As time passed, the memory of that traumatic encounter faded until one day Lisa excitedly announced that she had started bleeding before me, even though I was supposed to start first because I was older. Skeptical, I asked her to prove it. She tugged up her "pop top" an inch or so, rolled down the waistband of her peddle pushers, and showed me a small scab. It was well within the area our mother had indicated with her circling motion so Lisa figured it counted.

By this time, I'd figured out what Mom had probably intended to say and, feeling quite smug with my superior knowledge, I laughed and told her the scab was the result of scratching a mosquito bite until it bled. Then I corrected her ignorance by telling her that the place she needed to be watching for blood was her belly button. That was obviously the reason we had that little dent in our tummies, I informed her.

TMI

Fear, in this case exacerbated by ignorance, can jump up and bite us when we least expect it. Had we been able to grasp the "facts" of the "facts of life" our modest-to-the-point-of-prudish mother felt compelled to share with us, we might have been slightly scared, but we would not have been terrified. As it was, we were thrown into a state of dread regarding our future because of TMI—too much innuendo! Poor Mom. Life had not equipped her for such things and, as far as I know, Lisa and I, her fifth and sixth children, were the only ones she ever attempted to enlighten. It was the mid-1960s and she was probably panicked by what she was hearing on the radio about "love-ins," wife-swapping, divorce, and the sexual revolution of that era.

As children, our imaginations ran away with us pretty quickly, and terror was always only a heartbeat away. Sadly many adults haven't learned to harness that runaway fear response. Ted Kuntz, a therapist with a master's in counseling psychology, writes, "When confronted with a situation where the outcome was unknown, I noticed I often responded by imagining the worst possible outcomes."[1] The human penchant for making mountains out of molehills is like adding rocket fuel to our fear. "When I imagined the worst possible outcomes I experienced intense fear and anxiety. My heart would pound rapidly and my thoughts would race out of control. I noticed it was irrelevant whether what I imagined eventually occurred. Simply thinking a negative outcome caused significant emotional and physical distress."[2] Sound familiar?

Shocking News

I met Elva-Jean and Leon Brown in the mid-1990s when they, along with two other couples, moved to Ottawa, our nation's capital, to start a new church. I instantly liked the Browns, finding them both warm and approachable. They laughed easily but weren't afraid to be serious. I was saddened to hear, a few years later, that their marriage

was on rocky ground, and they had been let go from their church. I'll
let Elva-Jean tell the story.

After an exhausting day of taking care of three small children, I
was standing in the kitchen with the hot steam of dinner filling
the air as it simmered on the stove. The humidity was sweltering
but I stood there frozen and numb. After unpacking and sorting
through piles of dirty laundry from our family vacation to the
coast, I was exhausted. I was paralyzed by what my husband of
eight years just told me. Leon informed me that he didn't want to
be married anymore, and he especially didn't want to be married
to me. How can this be? The shock of hearing this was more than I
could handle. Eight years, three beautiful little children, and seven
years of ministry were evaporating as quickly as the steam from the
boiling carrots.

The minutes felt like hours. I stood there motionless, not sure what
to do, where to go, who to call. When did he start feeling like this?
And why was this happening to me? Rushing through my head
were questions I had no answer for. From the corners of my tired
eyes a little creek of tears soon turned into a waterfall. My life was
washing over a cliff, pounding onto the rocks below.

Fear washed over me. Following God in faith was a familiar concept for my husband and me. Every step we'd taken had been by
faith. We'd been active in Christian ministry almost from the start
of our marriage, and we'd even embarked on a church planting
outreach. Although our lives had been filled with uncertainty, we'd
been together and in harmony with God. But not now. This time I
knew the path in front of me wasn't going to be so easily navigated.
This time I was stepping out in fear.

Trying Not to Sink

After hearing the news, our church sent us to Christian counseling.
After several months the only thing that changed was that my husband moved further and further away from me. He was even more
convinced that he wanted out. He felt I was needy and insecure
and unable to stand on my own. At the end of our last session, the

counselor gave me the business card of a divorce lawyer and cautioned me to have a plan in place. The very next evening my husband took off his wedding band, tossed it on the table, and told me I had to leave.

With tears rolling down my cheeks, I picked up the ring I'd placed on his left hand eight years earlier and leaned it against our wedding picture on the mantel of the fireplace. Our circumstances were out of my control; my emotions were running so fast that I began suffering panic attacks. I was crying out to God every moment, "God, we followed You every day of our lives and now this! How was this part of Your plan? How can this be happening to us?"

After the local Christian counseling failed, we were sent away to intense counseling for ministry leaders and pastors. After extensive testing, evaluation, group counseling and private counseling, we went home with the knowledge that my husband was severely burnt out and moderately depressed. Two weeks later, we were "let go" from our church. As the days passed the depression became more severe. Leon became suicidal.

God's Promise

Every ounce of my energy was spent with God. I pleaded for my husband, for our young family, for our ministry, and for our lives. Then God spoke, "Wait patiently for the LORD. Be strong and courageous. Yes, wait patiently for the LORD" (Psalm 27:14 NLT). I suddenly had it—a peace that passes all understanding, a promise from God. I had to wait. I had to be strong and courageous. The enemy was not going to win. And I wasn't going to give up. I was waiting on the Lord. We were in a spiritual battle, and I was going to fight for my husband and family.

Our traditional wedding vows replayed every day in my mind: "In sickness and in health." Did that include spiritual and mental sickness? I knew this battle was God's. The enemy was not going to steal our ministry, kill my husband, and destroy our family.

The next 11 months, we lived apart. He moved his clothes and personal items to the basement, and the children and I lived on the third floor. We were unemployed, our savings were used up, and he had no place to go. He was waiting for me to walk out the door so he could blame me for departing and ending our marriage. I was too stubborn. God had given me a promise, and I was going to be obedient. Yes, I had to wait on the Lord.

We took a marriage course that lasted 14 weeks. It opened up lines of communication on issues we had to face. We finished the course with perfect attendance, but we were far from healing. Before reconstruction of our marriage could start we still needed to be broken. The old foundation needed to be removed, and the old mortar between the bricks had to be replaced. All we were left with were the old bricks. The Carpenter—Jesus Christ—needed to renovate our marriage and home.

On a Sunday morning while doing my devotions God directed me to a familiar verse in Isaiah 40:31: "Those who wait on the Lord shall renew their strength; they shall mount up with wings like eagles, they shall run and not be weary, they shall walk and not faint" (NKJV). "Lord," I said, "I am still waiting."

What I Longed to Hear

We headed off to the church at the opposite end of town we'd been attending because people didn't know us as we used to be. During the service the pastor asked if anyone had something to share about what God was doing in their lives. A few people said some things, and then as the pastor began his sermon my husband quietly stood up and said there was something he needed to say. All eyes were on him, waiting to hear what was so important that he'd interrupted the pastor. He started to talk, and the words just kept coming. It was like he hadn't spoken for two years, and now everything inside of him wanted to be poured out.

He put his hand in his pocket and took out his wedding band that he'd picked up from the fireplace mantel that morning. He held it up and told everyone that he took it off a year ago with no intention of ever putting it back on. He declared in front of the whole church how sorry he was for all the pain that he'd caused in my life. All I'd wanted was to hear him say three little words: "I am sorry." With tears rolling down his cheek, he said to me, "I am so sorry."

His words produced forgiveness in my heart. There was not a dry eye in church that Sunday morning. My husband declared his love for me and placed his wedding ring back on his finger.[3]

I Would Do It All Again

Elva-Jean had learned years before her marriage crisis to follow God. She and Leon had said yes to God's dream of full-time ministry and then church planting.[4] But learning to wait and trusting that God would restore her marriage was an impossible dream that could only be managed one *simple, immediate, possible* yes at time. Moment to moment, hour to hour, Elva-Jean took her fear to the Lord in prayer, and He gave her a promise (dream) from His Word on which to stand. Elva-Jean had this to share:

> Was all the pain, agony, and emotional roller coaster necessary? Yes, and I would go through it all over again to have what I have now. I am following God one yes at a time… even when He says, "Yes, wait patiently for the LORD."

Fear Scares Us!

"Fear—every woman struggles or has struggled with it in one form or another, and few dare to admit it. Why? We're afraid to!"[5] Grace Fox unveils one of the reasons this is true: People don't respect weakness, but strength. If women admit their fear, suddenly they become needy, clingy, insecure, just the sort of things Leon accused Elva-Jean of being in his rationale for wanting out of their marriage. Grace says, "Fear is our worst enemy. We can let it ruin us by filling our minds with thoughts of dread and woe, or we can face it head-on and use it as a tool that can empower us by drawing us into a deeper understanding of who God is."[6]

Fear can become a *barrier* behind which we cower, too afraid to say the next yes. Or fear can be the *pathway* on which we move forward, one yes at a time, perhaps slowly and painfully, but hand-in-hand with God. Every time we choose to believe God and say yes with our feet, a brick comes off the wall fear built and gets placed squarely in front of us to become a stepping-stone that takes us toward fulfillment of God's dream for us. How can fear be such vastly different things? I'm talking about *two* kinds of fear: *human fear* and *godly fear.*

Godly fear, writes Kathy Howard in her groundbreaking Bible study *Before His Throne,* is different from human fear:

> [Godly fear] is a spiritual attitude that will draw us deeper into our relationship with God...Although we normally view fear as a negative concept, the Bible, particularly in the wisdom literature, depicts the fear of God as a positive characteristic. In fact, God's Word makes it clear that fear is the proper response to a holy God.[7]

Godly Fear

With the help of a Bible dictionary, Kathy Howard defines *yare,* the Hebrew word for godly fear in the biblical text, as "standing in awe" or "reverence, whereby an individual recognizes the power and position of the individual revered and renders him proper respect."[8] Godly fear evokes faith; human fear revokes it. Godly fear calls forth trust in our almighty God, but human fear shakes our belief that God is able. We choose what fear we build with—one that puts up walls or one that builds roads. Elva-Jean chose godly fear over human fear as she waited, trusting in God's promises. I look back with deep satisfaction on times I've chosen to trust God and He has used my godly fear to overcome the barrier my human fear constructed. I recall with great disappointment the times I hid behind the walls my human fear threw up (with magical swiftness!), leaving the unanswerable "what if" questions ringing in my head.

Change "What If" to "What Now?"

"What if" questions can never be answered, can they? There are too many variables in any situations. People change, things change, times change—everything but God changes.

- What if I had said yes to that promotion?
- What if I had said yes to that other marriage proposal?
- What if I hadn't gotten into my car that icy morning?
- What if I hadn't resigned from that job?
- What if I had bought stocks in that upstart company?
- What if I had been more consistent in disciplining my children?

Continuing to ask "what if" only does one thing: It keeps you behind the barrier human fear has built. The minute you change "what if" to "what now," you are in position to hear from God, say yes with your feet, and move forward on the pathway of faith. Human fear builds walls; godly fear builds roads.

Peace Flies

A few hours after completing the first draft of the chapter on peace in this book, I found myself mired in misery. Peace eluded me as I grappled with human fear, my most common foe. I had just been made aware of a troubling situation in the life of someone I love, and my fear for her future created by my worst imaginings put up a barrier between me and God, between me and joy, between me and peace, between me and others. Barriers don't care who or what is on the other side. They keep every good thing out. Added to my concern for my friend was a new fear concerning me. *How can I write about peace when, in the blink of an eye, I lose mine so easily?* I thought. Suddenly I was experiencing the self-doubt all believers feel when our actions belie the truths we espouse.

Revisit with me the story of Peter when he stepped out of the boat and walked atop the stormy sea toward Jesus. Peter's deep sense of reverence and awe for Jesus (godly fear) summoned forth the courage he needed to leave the security of the vessel he knew could keep him from drowning once the sea was calm. His godly fear quelled the human fear that the surface of the water wouldn't hold him. When he stepped out onto the water with Jesus, Peter trusted in his heart that Jesus would help him. Human fear would have kept Peter in the boat; godly fear gave him the courage to step out in faith.

Triumphant to Terrified

Peter hadn't taken many steps when he *imagined* how precarious his situation was. He panicked and began to sink. In the blink of an eye Peter went from triumphant water walker to terrified sinking screamer: "Lord, save me!" he cried.[9] What did Jesus do? "Immediately Jesus reached out His hand, caught hold of him, and said to him, 'You of little faith, why did you doubt?' "[10] And that's the way Jesus still works in our lives today. He reaches out to us to save us.

The morning after my peace was stolen by fear and put out of reach by the barrier fear had erected I woke up still feeling anxious. I was so quiet on the 30-minute drive to church my husband asked what was troubling me. I confessed the catalyst for my unease and then bemoaned the fact that I felt unqualified to write about peace. Gerry reminded me that what I was going through was the most common affliction believers in Christ face in their daily lives: reconciling what they know as truth with what they experience as reality. Even though it helped to know I had something as common as the cold, it didn't fix the problem. I wanted a cure—not a shared hanky.

When we got to the community center where our young church meets, we got busy helping other volunteers haul tables and chairs and set up cooking grills in preparation for our first "Stampede Breakfast." Our church is in Calgary, Alberta, and every summer during the 10-day rodeo extravaganza called the Calgary Stampede, hundreds of thousands of people worldwide come to our city. There are free breakfasts all over the city and in the surrounding towns every morning. The typical menu is pancakes, sausage, coffee, and juice. Since our church had only recently moved to this larger community center, we had never hosted a Stampede Breakfast before and had no idea how many would come so we were prepared to feed 2500 people. Volunteers were already bustling when Gerry and I pulled into the parking lot shortly after seven o'clock on Sunday morning.

Working Partners

From one of our Filipino churches, several people showed up in cowboy boots, head-to-toe denim, and Stetsons to help us with the breakfast. One of the women has the same name as my younger daughter, and we'd met on a few occasions. We greeted one another warmly and began working side-by-side, taping large garbage bags to the ends of every row of tables that had been covered with bright plastic in the parking lot behind the community center. It promised to be a beautiful day as we chatted, catching up on each other's lives. She shared her concerns regarding her teenaged daughter, and it occurred to me that we were in the same boat—Peter's boat! But since, along with the terrified Peter, I was also sinking at the moment, I didn't have much to say. I didn't need to. Her next words pointed the way.

"I've been *living* in Philippiansh four, shiksh and sheven," she said, trying to talk while ripping off a chunk of duct tape with her teeth and sticking it onto the large black bag I had draped over the end of the table. Unsticking the tape from her dry lips, she repeated, "I've been *living* in Philippians 4:6-7. I even printed those verses on cards and stuck them everywhere in my house and even in my car." I looked up from my work and into her face. Jesus was reaching out to me across the stormy sea of human fear. He was speaking to me through the words of this fellow struggler, my sister in Christ. Would I take His outstretched hand? "Yes, Lord," I whispered in my soul.

My "little faith" was suddenly bolstered as I called to mind that passage I had long ago memorized and not thought of during the previous hours: "Be anxious for nothing, but in everything by prayer and supplication, with thanksgiving, let your requests be made known to God. And the peace of God, which surpasses all comprehension, will guard your hearts and your minds in Christ Jesus" (NASB).

Helped into the Boat

Although I was sinking a moment before, suddenly I was held in the hands of almighty God as He helped me into the boat. The storm of my circumstance still raged; nothing about which I was worried had changed. What changed was me. I went from drowning in human fear to standing on godly fear. The peace I felt "surpasses all comprehension"—especially mine.

When you see the hand of Jesus reaching out to you in the midst of the storm, grab it! Say yes to godly fear and trust Him. Then you'll watch the barrier of human fear fall into a heap of rubble at your feet. This is how God transforms our barriers into pathways. The bricks of human fear that we build our fortresses with come down just as quickly as the walls of Jericho collapsed in response to the godly fear of the Israelites who encircled the town and blew their trumpets and shouted at the appointed time.[11] My human fear, which robbed my peace, stole my joy, choked my faith, clouded my thinking, upended my emotions, tightened my shoulders—essentially doing everything but kill my appetite, darn it—was a barrier between joy and me, between peace and me, between God and me, between the life He wanted to give me and me. Once I grabbed hold of Jesus' outstretched hand, my human fear changed to godly fear, and I moved forward in faith on the path of peace. I could laugh again, breathe easily again, reach out to others again, live free again.

12

PRIDE

⁓⟡⁓

*Be who you is, because if you is who you ain't,
you ain't who you is.*[1]

LARRY HEIN

F our drivers, two keys, two cars. No matter how you add it up, this
situation equals frustration for the drivers. Our Volkswagen only
had two keys because no one took the time to get more keys cut. We
were too busy hunting for the two keys we allegedly had. This was
how life was when our daughters, now married, were still at home and
attending a university in Calgary, a half-hour away.

I was working at my desk one day when a cursory glance at the calendar revealed I had a haircut appointment in 15 minutes. I sprang
into action. Grabbing my purse, jamming my arms into my jacket, and
stuffing my feet into my boots, I lunged for the key rack and came up
empty. No key. I always hang my key on the key rack as soon as I get
home, but it wasn't there. I knew that one of the two keys was on my
husband's key ring, which at that moment was probably in his pocket
at his office. But where was the other one? The one all by itself on a
Free Willy key chain?

I ran downstairs to my daughters' bedrooms and began ransacking
Christine's room first (not that she'd notice since it already looked like
it had been recently vandalized). When I got to Anita's room I woke
her up because she had just worked a string of night shifts at a nursing

home and was sleeping during the day. Our encounter was not something I'd recommend in *Good Parenting* magazine.

"Where is the key to the Volkswagen?" I demanded.

"Mrrphh kublah, zzzz."

"Do you have my key to the Volkswagen somewhere in this disgusting mess?" I began flinging clothes aside in an effort to find the floor and, perhaps, the vagrant key.

"I didn't drive the Volkswagen last, Mom, you did…[yaaawwwwn]…now can I please go back to sleep?"

"If I drove the car last, the key would be on the key rack where I always put it!" I righteously announced.

Sitting up in bed with tears spilling over, my daughter reminded me she hadn't slept properly for a week, and now that she was fully awake, she probably wouldn't be able to fall asleep again. Begging me to leave her in peace, she assured me she had nothing to do with the lost key. I huffed and puffed and blew her room down anyway. No key. She covered her head with her pillow and cried herself back to sleep.

Free Willy Makes a Run for It

By now I was hopelessly late but angrier and more determined than ever. I called my husband, and he came dashing home to my rescue. Tethering his white steed outside, he rushed in to the foyer where I waited, ready to run the minute he "passed the baton." Working frantically to remove his Volkswagen key from the ring something shiny caught his eye and stopped him cold.

"What's this?" he asked. He walked over to the key rack, bent down and picked up Free Willy from the floor directly below it. "It looks like Willy tried to make a break for it." The twitching of his lips and twinkle in his eye betrayed the fierce inner battle that was raging. For the first time in 23 years of marriage, he had found something *I* had lost. Typically, Gerry loses his keys, wallet, and glasses about once a day. During a week at a conference center the year before, his wallet had been turned in to customer services no less than three times. But I digress. (My husband would call this "the old marital smokescreen.")

When Gerry loses things, he never bothers to look he just asks me because I always know where they are. Now, at last, he had the sweet taste of justice in his mouth since the tables were turned. One look at me warned him this was not a good time to celebrate. I burst into tears and refused to be comforted.

When Good Kids Happen to Bad People

"I am the world's worst mother!" I wailed as my husband reassured me over and over that it wasn't so. I managed to get a grip on my emotions long enough to thank him, briefly, and hurry off to my haircut. For the next hour I was seated in front of a vast mirror and had to stare into the face of the person I hated most in the world: Me! The World's Worst Mother! *Why do I always blame others?* I wondered.

On the way home from the haircut I stopped in at the grocery store to buy gifts for Anita to assuage my guilt. I ran into a friend, who listened as I poured out the whole saga and wiped my eyes repeatedly. Trying not to smile, she hugged me and reminded me that this was an isolated incident not big enough to dismantle 20 years of dedicated mothering. Slightly mollified but still shaken, I went home to set up two 12-packs of diet cola and three 10-dollar coupons for pizza like a shrine outside the sleeping daughter's door. Atop this was a note confessing the truth and begging forgiveness. I left again to run several more errands.

By the time I returned home hours later, ready to grovel, my daughter was already gone to work. She had torn the corner off my wordy note and scrawled a little message for me. She left it on the foyer floor where I would see it as soon as I came in. Her words demonstrated God's grace and her lovable, wacky personality:

> Hey mom, all is forgiven. As a matter of fact, you can yell at me again tomorrow. This could be a lucrative enterprise! xoxoxo.

Pride Knows "I'm Always Right"

Pride has many faces, but one of them is surely the "I'm always right" face. Life is so simple when you're always right. You never have to wonder if you're wrong because it's always somebody else. You never have to gather more information or do any research. Why clutter your mind with facts when your mind is already made up? You never have to say you're sorry, only "I forgive you" when the other person, who is seldom right, says she's sorry. You never have to change. Why alter perfection? You never have to ask for advice since you already know everything. Ah, the simplicity of always being right! I ought to know, I'm describing the natural tendency I have fought my entire adult life.

When I was expecting my first baby, do you think I asked my mother for advice? Of course not! I had a library card and a college education. She had only finished Grade 11 and then taken a dressmaking course. What could she possibly tell me that I didn't already know or couldn't discover in a book? Plus I had the sure knowledge that the way she did things when giving birth to her eight children was "yesterday's way," and time had marched on, bringing great enlightenment to the subject of childbirth and child-rearing.

How many doors have I slammed in the face of friendship, intimacy, shared dreams, and joint experiences because of pride? I shudder to think. This notion that we are so self-sufficient in what we know or where we choose to seek out information is based in pride.

During that nine-hour road trip that should have taken three hours that I alluded to earlier in this book, one of the passengers in the van repeatedly alerted me that I was on the wrong road. And she ought to have known the road since it was the road to the city where she'd grown up. When she noticed we were getting closer and closer to the mountains, which were to the west of where we were going, she sweetly suggested we may have missed a turn. (You tried, Karen!) We were supposed to be heading north on a road that ran parallel to the mountain range, so they should have remained always on our left, not straight ahead.

I Musta Missed a Toin at Albekoikee

I refused to listen. I was driving, not her. This was my van, not hers. I knew where I was going. Besides, if I needed to verify the truth of where I was, I would wait until I saw a road sign that indicated what highway we were on. Unfortunately there were no highway signs for almost two hours. On I went, stubbornly convinced I was right, while my traveling companions sweetly passed the time singing hymns in harmony from memory. When we finally came to a National Park kiosk in the middle of the highway and discovered we were about to enter Jasper National Park, I finally admitted I was lost.

"So how do I get to Edmonton from here?" I asked the person in the kiosk, hoping I could link up with the right road and redeem some of the lost time. No such luck. I had to go all the way back to where I'd missed the turn, take that turn, and continue on.

Just like my pride kept me from following the gentle prodding of the woman in the van who really did know where she was going, pride can hold us back from following God. Pride can be a barrier to saying yes to God if we stubbornly persist in going our own way, assuming we know what's best. Pride can keep us in an attitude of unforgiveness even though the Holy Spirit repeatedly prompts us with directives leading to freedom. But instead of listening for His *simple, immediate, possible* suggestion, we grip the wheel tighter and forge ahead.

Pride Has an Image to Maintain

Anyone with children knows that sometimes your kids can make you very proud. And sometimes they can make you want to sneak out of town in the dead of night. I met a woman at a conference who told me the most amazing story about life with her adopted son. She and her husband had children of their own but felt compelled to adopt a child from an underprivileged background. They raised him like their other kids, loved him, took him to church, and went to all his games. For the first dozen years, he made them proud.

Then it was like someone had pulled down the large handle that switches railroad tracks, sending the train onto a different set of rails. Her son headed off in a whole new direction the minute puberty hit. He smoked, stealing cigarettes or money to buy them. He skipped school, stayed out all night, and slept at his desk when he did go to school. The drinking started in earnest when he was 14, and after that he was never the same. He couldn't control his alcohol intake and would drink until he collapsed.

He was expelled from school many times until he was old enough to legally quit. The police were called often as he went further and further afield to steal the funds he needed to feed the monster of alcohol addiction. Years passed. He fell deeper and deeper into addiction. On more than one occasion, when all hope was lost, he locked himself in the bathroom of his parents' home and tried to take his life with pills or razors or drowning. Every time his life was miraculously spared. The police came repeatedly to their home, sometimes with sirens wailing in response to his crimes or his suicide attempts.

Pride Was Gone

"After a while," his elderly mother told me many years later, "all our pride was gone." The neighbors, the church, the business people—everyone in town knew her son, knew what a hopeless addict he was, and knew who his parents were. Whatever pride she had once had in being an upstanding citizen, a faithful church member, a wonderful neighbor, a loyal friend, a confident parent—everything was smeared with the brush of her son's irresponsible and out-of-control public behavior.

My heart broke as she described the situation. I expressed sorrow for all she had been through and all she had lost. Her response sent a current of electricity through me.

"Oh no!" she pleaded, reaching out to take my hand in hers. "Don't feel sorry for me!" Tears welled up in her eyes. "I am so grateful to God for all He has taught me through this experience. I've learned to trust Him. To lean on Him when all hope is gone. To get rid of stinking pride because it's not good anyway. No, no, no. I am blessed beyond measure for the gift of this son who helped me learn so much."

Time stood still as I tried to absorb what this godly woman, this woman who obviously *lived* at the feet of Jesus, was saying. She was grateful for the suffering she had endured. Instead of wishing she had never signed those adoption papers, she was completely convinced that her son had been sent from God to bless her. Even after all the boy had put her through. I was in awe. "Where is your son now?" I asked, thinking perhaps he had died and that would explain her attitude since one seldom speaks ill of the dead.

Chocolates on the Trail

No he wasn't dead. He was in a rehab program—again. Somewhere far away, and she was paying for the treatment as usual. He was doing great, she told me. He had been dry for more than a year and was preparing to be a leader in the program, hoping to help other addicts. Did she believe it would last? She *hoped* it would, even though nothing had worked before. But either way, she knew she could face what tomorrow held because she followed her Savior *one yes at a time.* This saintly woman had learned to lay her pride on the altar and let Christ squash it. In its place He filled her with Him. Every time she expressed gratitude and joy and blessing, I saw Jesus. It was a life-changing encounter for me as I noticed yet one more *chocolate on the trail* God gave me to savor as I followed Him.

Loved Despite Shame

Her story reminded me of something that had happened years earlier. Before saying yes to Christ at the age of 18, I was a troubled—and troublesome—teen. I became involved in narcotics and was arrested and charged with possession for the purpose of trafficking. I remember being in the car with my dad as he took me to court to appear before an itinerant judge for sentencing. As we pulled out of the driveway and onto the back alley that fed into the street, I tried to adopt a meek tone as I expressed my sorrow for damaging his reputation by my criminal activities. At the time, I wasn't sorry about the drugs—only sorry I'd been caught. But I did feel bad that in this small town where my dad had lived and worked his entire life, earning a reputation as a good, honest, Christian man, I would be the one of his eight children to bring shame on his name.

"You don't have to worry about *my* reputation," he replied to my apology. "I have my own reputation, and people know who I am. This doesn't hurt me. It hurts you. But you'll learn." He reached into his shirt pocket, pulled out his teeth, slipped them into his mouth, and then gave me a big smile. My dad was a class act!

Christ Humbled Himself

How many parents would worry about their image and not extend that kind of grace to their kids? Too many! How I wish my dad were still alive so I could express how grateful I am for his wisdom, his humility, and his unflagging hope that I would someday wise up and get on the right path. Paul wrote, "Do nothing out of rivalry or conceit, but in humility consider others as more important than yourselves."[2]

A few lines later, Paul writes about Christ's humility and exaltation. What he said, in my own paraphrase, is that Christ, being God, could have stayed in heaven—an eminently proud position—and clung to His Godness. Instead, He "humbled Himself by becoming obedient to the point of death."[3] And not just any kind of death but death on a cross, the most hideous form of agonizing torture the Roman machine invented.

Surely the opposite of pride is humility. The apostle Peter, a man acquainted with pride, as witnessed by his denial of Christ after His arrest, advises believers to "clothe yourselves with humility toward one another, because God resists the proud, but gives grace to the humble."[4] And God's grace was so evident in the face and life and words of the woman I met with the alcoholic son. She was the first to tell me that it was by grace alone that she came to a place of such peace, comfort, hope, and joy regarding her child.

Peter continues, "Humble yourselves therefore under the mighty hand of God, so that He may exalt you in due time."[5] The obvious message here is don't wait for life or circumstances (or your wayward kids) to force humility on you. Humble yourselves. The godly woman with the addicted son humbled herself. My dad humbled himself. Neither of these people are or were perfect, and they may have battled pride in other areas, but they found a way to be humble where it really counted—in regard to their children. What a gift for their kids!

Christ Humbled Me

I'd been struggling for a long time with a situation that had led to bitterness and unforgiveness. On a trip with Gerry and some friends, I finally realized what I needed to do. Kneeling in an upper room dedicated to prayer in a house of prayer last year in Jerusalem, I humbled myself before the Lord. He had a dream for me. A dream to free me from the bondage of unforgiveness, but I needed to let down my barrier of pride. In that room where I remained alone after my traveling companions had gone downstairs to enjoy the hospitality of our hosts, God spoke to my heart. He planted a dream and gave me a vision of what freedom looks like. Suddenly I saw and understood that as long as I held onto bitterness I was locked out from loving. The barrier of pride blocked my ability to love and receive love in many ways.

"Let it go," I heard in my heart. Such a *simple, immediate, possible* thing. Just let the negative emotions go. Unwrap my fingers from its throat, drop my arms, take a step back, and let the pain and bitterness go. I finally said yes. As I went downstairs and joined the others in the airy kitchen of the House of Prayer, I must have looked a bit like Moses coming down from the mountain after being with the Lord. His face shone so brightly he had to cover it with a veil because the glare was too hard on people's eyes.[6] Tears welled up when they asked me how I was. I quickly explained they were tears of joy, not sorrow. I had been with the Lord, and He had set me free. Together we had overcome the barrier of pride and love had rushed in to fill the place where unforgiveness had held sway for far too long.

Pride is a barrier. Whether it's keeping you from love, from friendship, from intimacy, from knowledge, from following God, if you hear God whisper into your heart three little words like "Let it go," say yes, drop your guard, and lower your arms. You'll be raising your arms again really soon, but it will be to embrace, not throttle.

13

GUILT

*They hid themselves from the L*ORD *God among the trees of the garden. So the L*ORD *God called out to the man and said to him, "Where are you?"*

GENESIS 3:8-9

After returning from our honeymoon at the lake in mid-August, I had to act fast to get ready to begin teaching a new grade level in a new school. Knowing that once classes started I wouldn't come up for air for 10 months, I felt pressured to get all my thank-you cards for wedding gifts sent out before the first day of classes. I set to work with diligence. I placed the large basket of gift cards, thank-you cards, and pens on the kitchen table and set a goal of completing 20 a day during the little breaks I took from working on the new fall curriculum. I was sailing along pretty nicely, sometimes surpassing my goal, writing entire paragraphs in each card to express our gratitude for the giver's generosity as well as our pleasure at seeing them at the wedding. Then I came to the card from my cousin Joan.

Inside each card, my sister Lisa as my only bridesmaid, had carefully written the precise contents of each gift so I would know what we had received and be able to thank them appropriately. I picked up the card from Joan and her husband, Roger, and smiled as I reread the sweet congratulatory message she had written. Then I looked for Lisa's distinctive loopy script and read: hibachi. Nothing more. Suddenly I remembered unwrapping that very gift to reveal a box picturing a small, camp-size barbecue and saying to Gerry, "Let's take this along on our honeymoon at the lake, and we can have our own little barbecue at our rental cottage." He agreed. We were delighted. But in the chaos of dashing off for our getaway, we forgot the hibachi. It remained with all the other gifts.

As I pondered what to say on Joan's thank-you card I was struck with the notion of how pleased she would be to know we had used her gift immediately. In fact, it had been the very gift that had "made" our camping trip! I imagined her squeal of delight as she read my story of how incredibly useful this hibachi had been to us. Knowing full well that I was doing something wrong, I wrote a big fat lie in Joan's card. Guilt hit me the minute I finished it. I pushed it aside with rationalizations of how happy Joan would be, sealed and stamped the card, and mailed it later that day, along with the others (all truthful) that I had written.

Guilt Comes Home to Roost

The lie haunted me whenever I thought of it over the next several months, but because Joan lived in another city and we weren't in the habit of communicating except at family weddings or funerals, I pushed the guilt away and eventually forgot about it. The following summer, after an exhausting-but-rewarding year of teaching, I started the holidays by taking out all the summer supplies we had received as wedding gifts but had never had time to use. From a high shelf in our storage room I pulled down the picnic basket, the patio lights, the barbecue tools, the lawn chairs and, in its sealed box, the hibachi. *Finally,* I thought with some relief, *I can use this blasted barbecue and make an honest woman of me! Sort of...* The guilt returned, and I flushed it away with my flimsy rationale.

I lugged things out to the kitchen and decided to open the hibachi box and get it set up so Gerry could see it when he got home from work. Perhaps I would even have time to buy some charcoal briquettes and a few burgers so we could enjoy our first barbecued meal of the summer. I placed the box on the countertop, fished in the cutlery drawer for a paring knife, and then sliced through the layers of clear packing tape. Lifting the flap, I reached inside expecting to grab a metal framework.

My hands encountered Styrofoam packing chips, which I had to clear away before I could see a heavy glass bell sitting atop a smooth wood cutting board. Taped to the board was a cheese knife. I pulled it out of the box and stared in disbelief.

Surely Your Sins Will Find You Out

The very next week I heard from Joan that she and her husband had bought a hotel in the nearby city where I was employed as a teacher. They were moving to my neck of the woods! Wasn't that great? I had mixed feelings of dread and shame, along with my excitement that they were going to be close enough to visit occasionally. Sure enough, they moved in, and we welcomed them. The Holy Spirit reminded me from time to time that I had a little "housecleaning" to take care of—confess the lie and ask for forgiveness. I was so embarrassed I couldn't bring myself to mention it, and Joan didn't say anything either. What I did instead increased my guilt. I avoided her, fearing the possibility that the "hibachi caper" might come up. I didn't pursue a closer friendship with this older cousin whom I had always loved and admired from a distance. I lived my life, she lived hers, and before long both of us had moved to different cities and the opportunity was lost.

About 15 years later, in a different province, I met and became friends with a fellow homeschool mom who happened to be my Cousin Joan's daughter-in-law. Her son and my son enjoyed many of the same activities, so we spent a lot of time together. Before long, Joan and Roger came to visit their children and grandchildren, and since we were nearby, they were nice enough to call us and ask us to join them. Once again guilt over the unconfessed lie rose up. I tried to stuff it down, thinking surely after all these years the statute of limitations on this lie has run out. Apparently not, because once again I felt like the lie was a barrier between us—not for Joan, but for me. She was as warm and loving and complimentary and encouraging and humorous as ever, but I felt a barrier between us, holding me back from fully enjoying her friendship. First there was the "crime," and then there was the cover-up for the crime. And the cover-up was continuing to inflict damage to our relationship.

The Moment of Truth

Finally I couldn't stand it anymore. On one of Joan's trips to visit her grandkids we found ourselves standing side-by-side enjoying her daughter-in-law's yummy cooking. I brought up the subject of the hibachi.

"Um, Joan?"

"Yes, my dear," she said smiling and turning toward me before taking a bite of her sushi hand roll.

"Do you remember…um…the wedding gift…er…that you gave me—the…ahh…the hibachi?" My mouth was dry and I was trying to keep my voice from quavering.

"Ah!" she exploded into laughter. "You Cavanaugh girls are *so* funny! Yes," she continued between chuckles, "Roger and I laughed our heads off!"

I stood there, speechless, just as stunned as I had been the day I pulled the cheeseboard out of the hibachi box. I had been skittish around my cousin for 15 years because of my lie, and the whole time she thought I was kidding! I completely lost all my courage, mustered up a squeaky laugh of my own, and joined her in the humor of the moment.

"Oh yes, we do love to joke around," I commented feebly. The kids dashed in from outdoors right then, hungry and boisterous, and the subject was dropped. (Yes, I did eventually come clean with Joan.)[1]

Guilt As a Barrier

Besides revealing my obvious need for daily grace, this story illustrates how guilt acts as a powerful barrier. What is guilt? This emotion comes when we think we've done something that falls short of our moral standards. Or, conversely, we have failed to do something we should have. If you are a Christ-follower, those standards are laid out for you in the Bible. Thus, honking your horn in irritation on your commute or forgetting your anniversary or flirting with a married coworker or eating grapes out of your grocery cart before going through the checkout may make you feel uneasy inside, like things are not quite right, that you have somehow failed. There is a reason for this.

As we travel along life's highway, interacting with God and others, we occasionally do things we regret. When we sin, God's Spirit, alive inside the heart of every believer, causes us to be troubled. Guilt is not solely a Christian experience; people who are not Christ-followers but are trying to live with integrity will feel pricked by their consciences when they break their personal code of conduct. Guilt is no respecter of persons; it is latent in everyone. (We were all created in God's image, after all.) When we know we have acted in a way that does not honor God or respect others, we feel guilty. Guilt acts like a fallen tree across the road of life. Until we deal with that obstacle, it will impede our progress. Guilt prevents us from going places we could go, experiencing things we could enjoy, and being with people we want to see. As my hibachi story revealed, guilt can prevent people from developing a deeper friendship. I'm sure we all know people whose marriages were damaged or destroyed by guilt. Guilt builds walls that we hide behind in shame, until we confess and find the unencumbered route Christ wants show us. Instead of taking our chainsaw in hand and cutting right through the log that is blocking our path, many of us look for detours or simply sit down and wait for the log to rot. I did both with my cousin Joan. I went the long way around, missing many chances to build a closer relationship. I kept silent for years hoping the guilt would just disappear, decomposing over time. The chainsaw that cuts through guilt is the decision to say yes and follow through when God whispers, "Confess."

That awareness of having disappointed yourself, others, and God leads to the flipside of the guilt coin wherein you assume you must be a bad person in order to have done (or thought) or failed to do something. "This concept of 'badness' of self is central to guilt."[2] Once you move from "I'm guilty" to "I'm bad" the dominos begin to fall more quickly. From there you can quickly feel, "I'm worthless," "I'm shameful," and "I'm scared." Shame comes from thinking that if others really knew you and how bad you were, they wouldn't want to have anything to do with you. And fear is the result of worrying that there might be some payback waiting around the next corner. Maybe the guy you honked your horn at will jump out of his car at the next stoplight and come after you with a tire iron.

When I'm feeling like a bad person—unworthy, ashamed, afraid—the last person I want to face is a holy God. Talk about a contrast. The glare of His purity makes me want to duck my head, cover my eyes, and slink away to lay low for a while until, hopefully, I feel a little better about myself because time has passed or I've done something to mitigate the "badness," such as taking cookies to crossing guards or walking the dogs at a local animal shelter. Sounds crazy, eh? You and me and a whole lot of other people punish ourselves with this kind of mixed-up thinking. We forget that we are saved from sin and self and death by God's grace (what *He* has done for us) and not by works (what *we* try to do for Him).[3]

So at a time when we need God most, we're avoiding Him! Our loving God wants to remove our guilt and replace it with godly remorse. Remorse targets the *behavior*, not *self* (our essence) like guilt does. For example, all children misbehave. But with the help of good parenting, behavior can be changed, improved, refined. It is the same with God's children. God wants to help you and me improve our behavior, to become more like Christ. He doesn't want to crush us under a needless weight of condemnation or hopelessness. Remorse is the proper conclusion that we have *acted* badly, not that we are bad.[4] Even though I may still feel bad about my bad behavior, I can take those feelings to God and ask Him for help to improve my behavior one yes at a time.

Please don't forget that as a child of God you have been forgiven *all* your sins—past, present, and future. In God's eyes you are completely righteous, totally clean, good enough for heaven through Jesus Christ. As long as we remain on earth we will sin, but we won't ever be rejected by God. Christ's death and resurrection on the cross guarantees it. The Bible tells us that nothing can separate us from the love of God that is in Christ Jesus our Lord.[5] If Jesus is your Lord—you have asked Him to forgive your sin and come into your life to rule and guide—then "nothing" means not anything, not even bad behavior.

Not all obedience (saying yes) leads to laughter and fun. Sometimes following God one yes at a time leads us to godly remorse. And this godly remorse can be painful. Knowing we have acted badly doesn't feel good. It hurts and we don't like pain. The fear that God is going to ask us to do something difficult or embarrassing or painful, such as confessing, can be a barrier that keeps us from wanting to go to Him.

And the barrier of guilt can grow as logs of fear, shame, and unworthiness fall on top of it. The longer we delay going to God with our guilt, the bigger the barrier grows and the harder it gets to clear away. The sooner you turn to God for help, the less lumber you'll have to cut through to continue onward toward realizing the dreams He has placed in your heart. The benefit of following God through remorse is that He uses remorse to refine us and remind us the next time we're tempted to sin what the cost is. God is more interested in making us holy than He is in making us happy. Thankfully, holiness brings its own rewards—happiness being one of them.

The Coffee Coupon Caper

A couple of years ago I clipped a coupon from our small-town newspaper for a "buy-one-get-one-free coffee latte." I carried it into the coffee shop listed in the ad, hoping that "coffee" was a generic word meaning "hot drink" as I planned to order something simple like a "grande soy milk chai tea, extra hot, no water, no foam latte" as my free drink after buying my friend's coffee latte. I happened to get the business owner as my barista, and when I displayed my coupon and confidently expressed my hopes, she flatly refused.

"Coffee means coffee," she said.

"Even though the free drink I want is cheaper than a second coffee latte would be?" I asked sweetly, hoping she would reconsider.

"No." Her one-word reply, without a smile, tipped the scales.

I thanked her, put the coupon back in my purse, turned away, and informed my friend we would be having our "date" at another coffee shop. I sailed out feeling miffed but justified. For the remainder of that day I was convinced that the shop owner's narrow thinking was "bad business."

Call Waiting

Early the next morning the Holy Spirit was able to get through to me. He may have been trying to get to me right from the start, but my attitude blocked all incoming calls. Self-righteousness is also a barrier. The inner exchange began as soon as I woke up and answered the call.

What did the coupon advertise—free coffee or free tea?

I know it said coffee. But come on! Work with me. What's the difference? They're both hot drinks.

Did that store owner have the right to deny your request seeing that the ad only promised coffee and not tea?

I guess so. But I'm a regular customer. I bring in a lot of business.

Did she deserve your haughty reaction after simply reinforcing what the advertisement clearly stated?

She could have smiled.

Take her flowers.

Ouch. One simple, immediate, possible yes to consider. Go back to the coffee shop with flowers? What will I say?

I already knew the three little words I needed to say. I was stalling. Just in case I lost my nerve at the last minute, I penned my remorse in a blank card, explaining that I was the lady with the coupon who had flounced out the day before. (I keep a hefty stock of blank cards on hand. My husband once suggested making an apology form letter to save time. I deeply appreciated his sensitivity regarding my busy schedule but informed him rather primly that each case *is* slightly different.)

Mea Culpa

As soon as I could, I drove downtown, bought flowers, and went to the coffee shop. The owner wasn't there. *Whew!* The barista of the day told me her boss was caring for her ailing elderly mother, as she did most days, and would only be in to cash out at the end of the day. *Ouch!* I took the note out of my purse, tucked it into the bouquet, and handed it over the counter with a short explanation: "I came in yesterday and acted like a jerk. Please give these flowers and my apology to the owner."

I left with the sad awareness that even though an apology helps, it is a poor replacement for godly behavior. At a time when that owner could have used a smile or a kind word, I had let her down. I had also let God down. I was feeling godly remorse.

Guilt for the Little Things

The reason I've used these two examples (the hibachi lie and the coffee coupon) in our discussion of guilt as a barrier to following God is because these are the everyday sorts of happenings that we feel guilty about. The "little things," relatively speaking. Things like rude behavior, unkind thoughts, white lies that lead to great big cover ups, forgotten birthdays, and missed opportunities to bring cheer to someone's day. Most of us aren't plagued with guilt for horrendous crimes or grievous acts. We haven't committed serious, life-threatening acts or outlandish behavior. We haven't embezzled funds from a humanitarian organization even though the offering plates pass right through our hands every Sunday morning. No, most of us deal with guilt in small helpings. But large or small, guilt has the same effect. It litters the path in front of us with twigs, branches, and fallen trees the size of Redwoods for us to trip over or hide behind.

Good Guilt; Bad Guilt

Guilt, like cholesterol, can be good and bad: one type of cholesterol clogs our arteries and hurts our hearts; the other one clears our arteries and helps our hearts. Guilt is like that. Good guilt drives me to God; bad guilt keeps me away from Him. Some people disagree, saying that instead of good and bad guilt, there is guilt, which is bad, but there is conviction, which is good. They believe guilt comes from the enemy (Satan), and conviction comes from our Lord and Savior, (Jesus). Whatever you believe, I say treat guilt and conviction the same way. If you feel convicted, go to God. If you feel guilty, go to God.

Look to God for a *simple, immediate, possible* yes that will cut through the barriers and allow you to go where God wants you to go. And when He whispers something as simple as "take flowers" in your ear, head to the florist without delay.

SHAME

*The central truth of the gospel is that
God forgives believing sinners.*[1]

The very thing I have always liked about living in small towns—that people know one another—can also be a problem if you suddenly act like an idiot. There is a certain sense of accountability that comes with knowing your neighbors that keeps people civil. There is no horn honking at our town's few traffic lights if the fellow at the front of the line is daydreaming and doesn't shoot forward the instant the light turns green. Road rage doesn't exist in our little burg. And chances are, if you did express your impatience in an outburst, you'd be hollering in the face of your kids' kindergarten teacher. People generally behave themselves and smile and wave when little social bumps occur.

Yes, small-town living has always been my choice. Until the day a type of insanity gripped me and I did the unthinkable. In response to the beginning of a growth spurt that eventually took our town from a population of 4000 to more than 16,000, a second grocery store was added. It was much bigger than the little store that had held a monopoly for decades. The new store offered something wonderful I had never heard of before: coupon days twice a month. The best coupon they offered was 15 percent saved on every $100 spent. I quickly figured out that if I ran my $300 worth of purchases through the checkout in three equal batches, stopping and paying for each hundred with an attached coupon, I could pocket 45 bucks! That meant we could splurge and order pizza for supper—essentially for free, paid for by the money saved at coupon day. The miser in me did back flips every time I shopped on those big savings days.

One coupon day I went shopping with a long list, as usual, but there was an item on my list I had never purchased at this store before—underwear. Let me divulge a family secret. My mother was an incredible seamstress, as mentioned before. Even after her seven girls grew up, left home, married and had children, Mom continued to sew for us. Twice a year, we would receive a package in the mail containing beautiful outfits she'd made. Not only did they fit perfectly, they were stylish. Mom kept everyone's measurements listed (in pencil, of course) beside our names on a small piece of paper tacked to the wall near her sewing station. Inside this twice-yearly package she would also include accessories, such as a belt, some beads, and earrings. And tucked under the tissue paper, out of sight but never out of mind, she never failed to include a package of underwear. Don't ask me why she did this; we never knew, but we always appreciated this quirky little addition to her love gifts.

Manna from Momma

In my case, having married a minister who went to graduate school for several years, Mom's little gifts were like manna from heaven. I needed those packages. I began to count on them. It was one less thing I needed to include in my skimpy budget.

Sadly, when my mom passed away during my mid-30s, I had to start buying my own you-know-whats. On the fateful day of which I write, standing in the small apparel section of the grocery store, I saw that my preferred brand was sold out. But since it was coupon day, my inner Scrooge decided to take a chance, buy the "house brand," and hope for the best. I grabbed two packages marked "M."

Not All M's Are Created Equal

Once I paid for my groceries and pocketed my savings, I went home happy. While hauling the groceries into the house and putting everything away, I hummed a cheerful tune. I planned what toppings

I would include on the "free" pizza we'd be having for supper. Going into my bedroom, I ripped open one of the two packages I'd tossed onto the bed moments before and pulled out what looked like a crib sheet. I picked up the package and checked the size. It was "M." *What does "M" stand for?* I wondered. *Magnificent? Maternity? Much much more?* I was expecting medium. Lies and fabrication (or was that fabric multiplication?)! I was steamed. Suddenly the happiness I'd experienced from the money I'd saved was canceled out by the purchase of something I knew I couldn't return. Or give away. I could just imagine which friend I would try to pass these off on. "Here's a little something you might use. They've never been worn, and they're brand-new. They don't fit me. They're w-a-a-a-a-y too big...but they should be perfect for you!" Now that's a relationship-ending conversation right there.

Now, here's where the insanity part comes in. Although I had read the "No Returns" sign in the clothing department, I grabbed my purchases and the receipt and went back to the store. The manufacturer had lied to me about its product, and I wanted justice...and a refund, sign or no sign. Unable to locate the woman who had served me an hour earlier, I chose the shortest line and inched forward until it was my turn. I placed the two packages, one open, one sealed, on the conveyor belt and said to the cashier, "These are not my brand, they don't fit, they're not the size they claim to be, and I want to return them."

"I'm sorry, madam," the cashier began, pleasantly enough. "Did you see the sign in the department? It clearly states there are no returns on..."

"I'm aware of that," I interrupted, not wanting to waste her valuable time on the busiest day of the month. "I read the sign. However, the size listed on the package is not the size of the item *inside* the package, and I believe I should be allowed to return them." The line behind me was growing, making both of us anxious. We went back and forth for a few more minutes, neither of us willing to budge. With a heavy sigh and a frown, the cashier picked up her "blow horn" and summoned the manager.

We waited. People with coupon-day carts piled like the Grinch's sleigh the night he stole Christmas, began to cut out and look for a quicker line. Mothers tried to calm cranky children. I apologized to those nearest me as we waited for the manager to arrive. Finally a rather harried-looking, not-even-shaving-yet young man squeezed in beside the sales associate and asked how he could assist me. We covered the same ground. I didn't budge on my position, convinced in my temporary madness of the rightness of my quest.

"Look," I stated through a clenched smile, speaking as rapidly as an auctioneer, "I came looking for my brand but you were sold out so I decided to buy *your* brand. But since there was no sample tacked up on the wall I had *no way* of knowing what size to buy so I bought 'M,' the size I take in *my brand*. But once I got home and opened the package, I saw that not all M's are created equal, which I don't think is quite fair since how else is one to know what size to buy if there are no samples for viewing. And I would *never* think of ripping into a package in the store and checking even though *many people* do that, but *I* don't think it's right." I took a breath.

The manager jumped in, and we covered the same ground I'd just gone over with the cashier. To no avail.

"But, madam, there...are...no...returns," the manager repeated for the final time, unwavering in his steely gaze.

Seeing Is Believing

I snapped. Grabbing the opened package, I pulled out the product and held them up in all their vast glory between outstretched arms. "I am no Tinkerbell, but does *this* look like a medium to you?" The people lined up behind me gasped in horror. The manager blanched.

"Give her a full refund," the stricken lad...er...manager whispered hoarsely to the cashier as he scuttled back to his office. Feeling absolved, I smiled sweetly at the cashier. She *did not* smile in return. She still had a little fight left in her.

"I'll refund you for the unopened package, but not the one you've ripped into." She began pounding on the proper keys to open the cash drawer. Still in the grip of my craziness, I leaned in close so I could share my thoughts privately.

"What do you think I did?" I asked, sotto voce. "Open the package, put them on, wear them all around town, go home, take them off, wash them, dry them, iron the creases back in, and bring them back for a refund—all in 45 minutes?" She stared at me for a minute longer as we stood, nose-to-nose, unflinching. Then she reached into her cash drawer, counted out a full refund for both packages and plopped the money onto the conveyor belt.

"Thank you," I said, feeling absolved. But as soon as the money was in my hand, the full import of what I had done rolled over me like a tsunami. Like Judas, I looked down at the "30 pieces of silver" and wanted to turn back the clock and start this day over. This was a small town. Many people knew me. What was I thinking? Shame hit me with stunning force.

My Story's Raison d'Etre

As a matter of fact, I am so ashamed of the way I acted that day that I've removed and put this story back in several times during the writing process. The reason it keeps coming back like telemarketers at supper time is twofold: in my writing as well as my speaking, I hope I never paint a picture of myself that is anything less than truthful. I am the worst of sinners and in grateful awe that God would stoop to love me. And second, in a chapter about shame as a barrier that hinders us from following God, this is an excellent example of its impact.

I've never returned to that grocery store to make amends. I avoided even going there to shop for several months. Finally, wanting to get back in on the coupon day deals, I cut and colored my hair, bought different glasses, and returned literally shorn and sheepish. I don't know if I would have had the courage to apologize to the cashier and manager because I never saw them again.

My behavior inside those walls for the next several years can only be described as pathetically pleasant. I straightened shelves, picked up stray items off the floor, helped other shoppers find wanted items, smiled at everyone whether I knew them or not, gave up my place in line without being asked, and was so sickeningly sweet to the cashiers they needed wet wipes to unstick their hands from my money after serving me...all in an effort to compensate for my horrid behavior.

And to make the situation worse, I found out just a few months ago that my next-door neighbor had been in the store that day (more than 10 years ago) with her children. They had witnessed the entire exchange. Although we are friends, she didn't reveal she'd been there until she heard me refer to the event with great remorse. At that point she admitted she'd always wondered what in the world I was thinking. All those witnesses to my temporary insanity. My testimony and witness for Christ sure suffered that day.

Shame As a Barrier

Shame keeps things hidden; transparency reveals. Shame covers up; transparency uncovers. Shame invites blackmail; transparency "scoops" it. Shame holds us back from fellowshipping with God because as long as we feel ashamed, we don't feel worthy to approach Him. God wants to take us, one yes at a time, from shame to transparency so that we can get back on track with being in close relationship with Him and pursuing the dreams He gives us.

Shame prevents some alcoholics from a full recovery because they balk when they get to Step 5 of the Alcoholics Anonymous 12-step program. What is this dreaded step? The need to share with another human being the "exact nature of our defects."[2] Why is this such a terrifying and humbling task. Because alcoholics and addicts are ashamed of things they've done in their compulsive quest to feed their disease.

I'm not addicted to alcohol or drugs, but I am addicted to sin. And as an addict, I have plenty of shame about things I've done. The reason AA includes this all-important fifth step is because AA's founders learned the hard way and observed in others that keeping secrets leads straight back to the bottle. Shame can be a barrier between us and recovery so we need to be transparent.

The Foamy on Loany

When Gerry and I had our first child we were so broke we couldn't even afford to buy her a crib, new or used. Fortunately, someone gave us a much-used crib that sanding and fresh paint rendered into a usable bed. However, the mattress that came with that crib was more than used—it had been "used up" and was ripped and tattered. Since it was all we had, I scrubbed it thoroughly, applied duct tape to the worst areas and wrapped a clean blanket around it before putting on the fitted crib sheet. But even after all this, it really bothered me to put my precious little child on top of that lumpy, saggy, torn up mattress. What kind of mommy puts her baby in such a substandard bed? I felt ashamed and hoped no one would ever peek under the sheets to see what kind of mother I was.

Brothers Without Borders

A few months later, we hosted a group of American Indians at our church. They had come from Arizona to help with our summer programs that reached out to Canadian First Nation's People. Our church had a nice kitchen, adequate bathrooms, and plenty of space for our visiting guests. All we lacked were beds. A sister church in a nearby city loaned us the use of their brand-new, four-inch foam mattresses. They were perfect: clean, firm but comfortable, and easy to stack and store when we used the "sleeping room" for church services.

After our summer guests returned south of the border, Gerry and I spent a few days cleaning and organizing things. Gerry stacked the mattresses where they could be collected by the pastor of the church that had loaned them to us. As I helped him stack them, it occurred to me that one of these mattresses was about the same width as our crib, but too long by a couple of feet. Saying nothing, I went and fetched a measuring tape from Gerry's tools and surreptitiously measured the top mattress once Gerry left to deal with other tasks. I walked across the property to our house and measured the crib. Bang on! All I needed to do was lop off a couple of feet and it was a perfect fit.

I hauled one of those foamies over to the house, cut off the extra footage, hid the remnant and carried the old mattress down to the basement. I placed the foam piece in the crib, covered it with the blanket and the sheet and carried on with my day. My baby had a new mattress. I felt like a better mommy. For a few hours anyway. When the glow of improved motherhood wore off, a prick of conscience was keenly felt.

How do you justify thievery as good mothering?

I'm not stealing it—just borrowing it. I'll glue the end piece back on and return it as good as new as soon as I'm finished with it.

Did you ask the owner of the foamy if you could "borrow" it and cut it up?

Come on! We needed it. My baby deserves better than what I was giving her.

Was it yours to take?

They'll never miss it. There's a whole stack.

To ensure the conversation ended, I turned on the radio and distracted myself with other chores. (Yes, I was a Christian and a pastor's wife at this time, not a juvenile delinquent even though my thought pattern suggests I was. What I did and was doing with rationalization was shameful.)

Busted

A few days later I got a call from the wife of the pastor from whom we'd borrowed the foamies. She had raised seven children herself on a budget so tight she couldn't spare the dime a cup of coffee at the café would have cost for most of those years. She understood penury. She would have gladly found a way to "loan" me a mattress had I asked. But since I didn't ask, her question after our opening pleasantries chilled me to the bone: "Are any of those foam mattresses we loaned you still there? We seem to be missing a few." From this I deduced rightly that I hadn't been the only one to pilfer from the stack in the last few days. I was filled with shame, and my face was instantly red. *Thank goodness she's not asking me face-to-face,* I thought. So what did I do? Shamefully, I lied.

"Um, no I don't think so, but I'll have a look around and call you back." I hung up the phone and wanted to run and hide in the deepest cave. But instead, thankfully, I looked up. God let me know the simple, immediate, possible yes I had to act on. *She's your friend. Call her and explain.*

I think if God had said "confess" instead of "explain," I would have backed off. I was so embarrassed and ashamed that confession seemed almost impossible. But explaining my thought processes to one who loved me and empathically understood my situation, that was something I felt able to do. I picked up the phone and called her back. As I explained what I had done, her sweet understanding and instant forgiveness called forth a full confession. I wiped tears of gratitude off my face as I hung up the phone after being assured by her that all was well between us. And it still is. Thirty-two years and thousands of miles later, this saintly mentor remains one of my dearest friends and prayer supporters as she nears her ninety-third birthday.

Leon's Story

Taking the lid off of shame to let in God's light results in the growth of beautiful things, including lifelong friendships. Spiritual renewal also grows in the light of transparency. Remember Elva-Jean and Leon, and how God assuaged Elva-Jean's fear with promises from His Word? Yes by yes, she continued to follow God and trust Him during those long dark months of marriage separation while in the same house. Even though Leon tried to make her leave him so the marriage breakup wouldn't be his fault, and she had every reason to do so, she stood on God's promises and He carried her through, moment-by–moment, until victory was assured. Here is Leon's perspective about how shame almost kept him silent when God told him to speak. But because he said yes to what God asked him to do one Sunday morning, his transparency created ripples that went beyond his own situation. When God gives us a dream and we say yes, He uses our simple, immediate, possible obedience to spread goodness and light well outside our own small circle of acquaintances.

Saturday morning, the day before the Sunday where Leon apologized publicly and put the ring back on his finger, he drove three hours from home in order to visit three people in Toronto. During the 18 months since telling Elva-Jean he wanted out of the marriage, Leon felt no love for his wife. The love that had been there for years and had fueled his pursuit of her had flown away, and he knew not where. No matter how hard he tried to bring it back or muster it up, he couldn't. However, something—his connection with his kids? God? Lack of direction and cash? All of these?—kept him from leaving the family home. And something kept him going to counselors and marriage classes with Elva-Jean for help. But nothing had helped so far.

On this Saturday morning he visited two people for advice: a fellow pastor and Elva-Jean's older sister. Now he was on his way to see a person for absolution—his mother-in-law. Leon and Elva-Jean had eloped against the wishes of her parents, especially her mother. The barrier this created between Leon and his mother-in-law had never been breached or even addressed. Leon knew God was asking him to do this, and he said yes. And God worked a miracle of forgiveness and healing between them—poignant, timely *proof* that Leon was on the right path.

The Hidden Switch

Driving home late that night, Leon said he felt like the switch that had been turned off, cutting off his love for his wife, had been turned back on. He was filled with so much love and desire for his wife he could hardly wait to get home. But God had one more simple, immediate, possible yes He wanted Leon to act on. He wanted him to wait until the next morning and, because their marriage troubles had been such a public issue, He wanted Leon to "tell the truth in church." Leon said yes, went home, and slept alone in his basement bedroom for the last time.

Sunday morning early, he slipped his wedding ring into his pocket when no one was looking and drove the family to the church they had been attending for several months. Leon had earned a reputation there of being the "strong silent type," with the emphasis on silent. People wondered if he was unapproachable. He hadn't made any friends there yet. All the way to church, in silence as usual, he battled to stay true to what he knew God had asked. He was so ashamed at what he had done to his wife, his family, his former ministry partners, his former church. He began to lose his nerve.

Words from the Heart

The service began and, as mentioned earlier, the pastor asked for people to share. Many people gave short testimonies and tributes about the greatness of God. Leon sat quietly. There was a moment of silence while the pastor waited to see if anyone else wanted to say anything. During that few-second interlude, a man who was seated beside Leon muttered under his breath that he "just wished somebody, for once, would stand up and say something real. Something from the heart."

Bingo! Leon recognized the hand of Jesus reaching out to him across the stormy sea. He stood up and the floodgates opened. There never was a message from the pulpit that Sunday morning. None was needed. People wept, and some confessed. Many came to Leon that day, and many times afterward, to say how God had used his transparency to give them the courage to say yes to God and confess their own shame, seeking forgiveness and restoration. Spiritual renewal swept through the little church and hundreds of lives were impacted.

Today, six years after that life-changing Sunday, Leon and Elva-Jean, following God one yes at a time, have reunited with their former ministry partners, mended broken relationships, and built new ones. Their marriage is on solid ground. Leon says his heart is filled with more than love for his wife. When she refused to flee the marriage, as he thought she would, and remained true to God and to him, she also earned his utmost respect.

God doesn't want to leave us in the dungeons we go to when shame puts its grip around our throats. He wants to lift our heads and bring us into the light of His love and forgiveness with hope. Transparency is the key that unlocks that dungeon door. Look to God! And if you hear something like "Go see your mother-in-law," start driving. Follow Him one yes at a time and watch what happens. Like He did with Leon, God may use your obedience and transparency to throw open the doors of spiritual renewal in your faith community.

15

COMPARISON

When Peter saw [John], he said to Jesus,
"Lord—what about him?"...
"If I want him to remain until I come," Jesus answered,
"what is that to you? As for you, follow Me."

JOHN 21:21-22

Barb's husband, Jim, got his paycheck from policing, but he got his thrills from fast cars. For years he was involved in every aspect of auto racing, spending most of his spare time getting ready for a race, going to a race, racing, or recovering from a race. When Jim worked his way up from the pit team to racecar driver, he couldn't wait to get out on the track and show his stuff. Unfortunately, his "stuff" didn't include winning. Worried he'd lose his place as a driver, Jim hired a coach to ride with him and help him improve his technique.

It didn't take long before Jim's coach diagnosed his problem. Over a cold drink in a nearby watering hole, the coach summed things up: "I can tell you right now why you're not winning races, Jim. I've noticed that it doesn't matter whether you're in second place or thirty-second, you always make the same mistake. You get stuck behind the car in front of you and instead of looking past him you watch his trunk. You'll never pass anyone with your eyes on the trunk. Take your eyes off him and look at the road ahead, and then you'll see your opportunity."

Not only did that bit of diagnostic wisdom improve Jim's driving—"After that I won lots of races and a few major Championships too"[1]—it changed his life. And Barb's. And mine. During a coffee chat with

Barb several years after Jim's racing days were over she shared his pearl of wisdom in response to my singing the "I'm not as good as her" blues. She didn't need to interpret the story for me. I got the message loud and clear: Get your eyes off her trunk!

Comparison cripples. As long as I'm watching some other person's trunk, I can't see the path God wants me to walk. I've got my face so buried in her capable "boot," to borrow the British term, I can't fathom being used or even wanted by God. Why would God want me? He's got her! And she's in front; she's winning. I'm not as good as she is. And as soon as I give in to those lies, my foot eases off the gas pedal and I fall further and further back, confirming what I already believe: that I'm a loser. Paul says,

> Let us *throw off everything that hinders* and the *sin that so easily entangles,* and let us *run with perseverance* the *race marked out for us.* Let us *fix our eyes on Jesus,* the author and perfecter of our faith, who for the joy set before him endured the cross, scorning its shame, and sat down at the right hand of the throne of God. Consider him who endured such opposition from sinful men, so that you *will not grow weary and lose heart"* (Hebrews 12:1-3 NIV).

Let me delineate Paul's points for you , and then we'll look at them individually.

- Throw off everything that hinders
- The sin that so easily entangles
- Run with perseverance
- The race marked out for us
- Fix our eyes on Jesus
- Do not grow weary and lose heart

These truths hold the keys to our first-place finish in God's eyes.

Throw Off Everything That Hinders

What is "everything that hinders"? Simply put, these are the barriers that come between God and us. Fear hinders. Guilt hinders. Shame hinders. Doubt hinders. Pride hinders. Comparison hinders. These walls keep us from following God in all areas. What hinders are attitudes, choices, behaviors, wrong thinking that hold us back from following God 100 percent.

A huge barrier for me has always been comparison. It throws up an obstacle as big as the back end of a Hummer (what a bummer!), behind which I wallow in defeat, convinced I don't have enough tiger in my tank to pass so why try?

The Sin That So Easily Entangles

There are things that do not tempt me—gambling, gluttony, golf. Unless I change, I'm unlikely to be entangled by any of them. Some of us pride ourselves because we don't drink, smoke, spit, or chew (or hang out with girls who do). We assume we've got it all together and nothing is hindering us from following God. But everyone has habits, weaknesses, attitudes, and recurring behaviors that continue to tie them up and hold them back.

Sometimes it's simply the lies we believe that entangle us. "I must be perfect before God can use me," is a powerful lie people buy in to. Worldly lies such as "Life should be easy" ensnare us by getting us to think, *Since I'm struggling, this must mean God doesn't care.* Distortion lies are "feelings equal facts" thoughts: If I feel like a loser, I must be a loser. Even spiritual lies abound: "God can't use me unless I'm spiritually strong."[2] Every one of these lies has the power to throw sugar in our gas tank, keeping us from embarking on our journey with God. This is what is meant by "the sin that so easily entangles." For you it might be fear. For another, guilt. Someone else, it's doubt. Perhaps shame is the stopper. The list of possibilities is as endless as the number of people on earth. Many people have more than one sin that easily entangles them. (Did you see my hand go up? I get entangled by all of the lies mentioned so far…and more. And every time I allow myself to become tied up, I'm kept from wholeheartedly following and serving God.)

Run with Perseverance

In my brief season as a runner, a running partner who had completed marathons prior to our association suggested we enter and run in some five- and ten-kilometer races (5K is approximately three miles, and 10K is approximately six miles). Cindy convinced me I could do it, so we began to train. With incredible patience she high-stepped along beside me, chatting while I gasped. She encouraged me every step of the way when we headed out in the early morning hours before my kids awoke. Cindy rode her bike across town to my house at six, and then rode home again because she knew that she wouldn't get enough of a workout by running with me. I managed to stagger one kilometer the first day and thought I would die. I didn't, unfortunately, which meant I had to run with Cindy again in two days.

Over a period of weeks, I slowly gained strength and endurance until we were running 5K three times a week. A few months into our training program, Gerry decided to join us. He hadn't done any running for 15 years. His first time out, he ran 10 kilometers. (Doesn't that just fry the hair right off your head? I wanted to slug him, but I couldn't catch him!) Cindy and I ran a couple of 5K races that summer, and the next year she decided we were ready for a 10K. I wasn't so sure. No matter how hard I tried, I couldn't seem to break the 5K barrier, even though we were running regularly. In fact, the first time I ran a full 10K was the day of the race!

A family emergency called Cindy out of town at the last moment, and I almost dropped out. But the weekend of the race, some relatives came to visit. On a whim, my sister-in-law, who claimed she never ran anywhere, decided to run along beside me. Her 15-year-old son joined in too. He didn't even have any running shoes or shorts in his suitcase, so he decided to go in blue jeans and leather loafers. The 10K race we entered was designed so that the first kilometer was level, followed by a four kilometer climb (1000 feet elevation gain), at which point we made a U-turn and ran back down for four kilometers and finished the final kilometer on level ground.

The gun sounded and off we went. We three stuck together, laughing and chatting on the level ground. Then we started to climb what's known in our valley town as the Big Hill. My nephew began to pull further and further ahead as he loped along easily in his street shoes, jeans, and hoody. His mom and I chugged our way up that hill with aching lungs and screaming thighs. We still had a kilometer to go to the crest when her son sailed past us, already on his way down. He had barely broken a sweat. On we went.

There weren't many people behind us as we climbed the Big Hill, and the last of them passed us as we made our way back down. After a while we noticed a persistent puttering sound behind us. Looking back we saw the race marshal inching along on his scooter, bringing up the rear (us!). We were dead last. He kept far enough back to preserve our dignity but close enough to be available if we collapsed.

On we ran. I use the word "ran" rather loosely, you understand. Plod would be more accurate. Sixty-three minutes after the starting gun sounded, my running mate and I "sprinted" (quit laughing!) over the finish line. In case your math is worse than mine that's a pace of 10 minutes per mile. It's a good thing I trained for two years! My nephew finished in 45 minutes and had time to wipe his moist brow and relax with a cold drink while he waited for us to finish.

I was incredibly proud of my accomplishment that day. I displayed my race number with the photo of my red-faced, finish-line grimace attached to it on the fridge for months. Why? Because my goal had been to *finish* the 10K race, not to *win* it. I didn't know whether or not I could make it twice as far as I had ever run before, and that day I proved I could. That run modeled for me one of the ways competitions can be good. As long as I was competing against myself instead of against the other racers, I was a winner. If I had failed to persevere and stopped running when I realized that, *by comparison*, I was slower than every other runner in that race, I would never have reached my goal. The next year I ran again, finishing dead last again but realizing my new goal of running a 10K in under 60 minutes. I made it with 13 seconds to spare! Go team! I don't run anymore. It's wise to quit when you're at the top of your game.

The Race Marked Out for Us

There is a *race marked out* for each believer. The big picture of what that looks like is in Paul's letter to the Philippians: the goal is to know Christ and become like Him.[3] Within that *overarching purpose* to grow into Christlikeness are many *overlapping dreams*, such as running 10K in under 60 minutes, reading the entire Bible in one year, raising $1000 for humanitarian relief, cutting a CD of original music, completing a university degree, and on and on and on. How do we achieve these dreams? By following God *one yes at a time.* Because God is personally involved in our lives, He has unique *plans* for each of His children. He has gifted each of us with different "running" styles, if you will. The way we run the "race marked out for us" that leads to Christlikeness and to all our other dreams is as distinct as our DNA. No two running styles are the same.

Does that mean no two people have the same dream? Of course not. It means that no two people will realize their identical dreams the same way. Two people might each dream of developing a business to have the freedom to invest heavily in God's work internationally. One person might become the founder of a national restaurant chain specializing in fried chicken, with the profits going to fund building orphanages in developing countries. The other owner may have a single hot dog stand that makes enough money to finance annual family mission trips. Same dream: business success finances humanitarian causes. Similar outcomes: one pays for orphanages, the other hammers the nails that builds them. Both businesspeople realized their *dreams* but with totally different running styles or methods: a national chicken chain and a single hot dog stand.

Fix Our Eyes on Jesus

If the hot dog businessperson in our example allowed the massive scale of the fried chicken co-runner to intimidate him (or her), he may have never even tried to run the race marked out for him. That crippling comparison would have hindered him and his family from the satisfaction of following God to realize His dream. Instead, when God gives us His dreams, we need to take our eyes off the "trunk" of the runner in front of us, look past him, "fix our eyes on Jesus," and persevere. Both times I came in last on those 10K runs I saw a lot of "trunks" that had a lot more jiggle than mine did, and they still beat me. Point being, even though I appeared to have a more "runnerly physique" than some of them did, when it came to the race, they proved to be in better shape and faster. Don't be put off by the outward appearances of others; they don't always tell the whole story.

You may think God has given you a dream you're not fit enough for. Just like those runners who carried a bigger caboose over the finish line than I did, they proved that it takes all kinds of people to make up a running field. If any one of them had taken a good look around the pool of runners waiting for the starting gun and compared themselves to the ones who looked sleeker and faster, they might have decided to stand down and not even try. That would have denied them the joy of watching runners like me stagger across the finish line—thinner, younger, rigged out in running gear, and dead last, just a few feet in front of the motor scooter.

Do Not Grow Weary and Lose Heart

Sometimes we just want to quit, don't we? After a day where the word count on the cutting floor doubled the word count on the page, I wanted to quit writing this book. Actually I wanted to quit writing, period. I wanted to quit public speaking too. Forever. I was done with words. I wanted to erase my website, change my name, get an unlisted number, and put an obituary in the paper that said glowing things about my life and mourned my untimely death. In my new life, I planned to put on dark glasses, pull a ball cap down to my eyebrows, and drop by the garden nursery in my town to ask for a job. With dirt. Not words. Not people. Not deadlines. I didn't care what the pay was.

Various things had brought me to this wanting-to-quit point, but the main one, the one that so easily entangled, was comparison. I thought, *There are already so many incredible writers and so much amazing material, who do I think I am trying to run the same race as them?* As I mentally scanned the field of runners, I felt like I had a lot more jiggle in my trunk than most of them! I began to doubt if I would cross the finish line at all. Or, if I did, how far behind all those faster, sleeker, younger, fitter, more suitably clad runners would I be? Around five o'clock that day, I closed my laptop, slouched alone over a supper of leftovers because my husband was out of town, and drove to the prayer and Bible-study group that meets weekly at Pat and Susan's house. Our teacher, Pat Duggan, is a successful entrepreneur and businessman in his fifties. By his own admission, neither he nor his wife finished high school. As a matter of fact, he left school and went to work after Grade 8. Leaving school didn't end Pat's education; it started it. He is a lifelong learner with more than one trade and many business ventures under his belt.

Pat began the evening's study with a large three-ring binder in his lap. Inside that binder was 200 pages of material he'd prepared that covered the first seven chapters of the book of Romans. "That's as far as I've gotten," he said. When we completed our group study of the book of Acts the week before, Pat was already way ahead of us. He'd been working on Romans for months. He led our group to dozens of scriptures in his opening remarks about this amazing letter Paul wrote to the church in Rome. It was fascinating. The time flew by, and before I knew it we were closing our eyes for prayer.

On the 30-minute drive *to* the Duggan's house, I'd decided to ask for prayer regarding my desire to quit speaking and writing and my intention to work with dirt. But Pat's teaching had been so inspiring and God's Word had been so comforting, I'd forgotten my prayer request. Several of the scriptures we read reminded me of my own "Damascus Road beginnings" with Jesus and His dream for me to follow Him as a writer and a speaker.

Not only was I inspired by God's Word and Pat's excellent teaching, I was encouraged by Pat's life. Sitting in front of me was the embodiment of the message of this book! Pat's success is the direct result of all the yeses he has said to God for the last 20 years:

- Yes, I will quit living for the bottle.
- Yes I will start living for You.
- Yes I will leave this successful trade and start up my own company in a whole new field.
- Yes I will love and pray for my kids who do not follow You.
- Yes I will absorb the cost of this accident to my new SUV

because the young woman who caused it said she'd lose her insurance if I reported it to my insurance.

- Yes I'll preach when the pastor is away even though it takes me months to prepare.

- Yes I will study and teach the Bible even though I've never had any formal training.

- Yes I will love my wife in such a way that no one will question it.

- Yes I will dedicate my time and energy to the administration of our church because the pastor also has another full-time job and he needs my help.

So many yeses, and every big yes made possible by thousands of simple, immediate yeses each and every day.

For an hour that night as Pat taught and we prayed, I was able to fix my eyes on Jesus, the author and perfecter of my faith. Before we said "Amen," I heard God say, *All I'm asking is that you get up tomorrow morning and show up at your desk. Will you say yes to that?* One *simple, immediate, possible* yes. By the time I left Pat's house, I was changed. I had hope. I got up early the next morning and went to my desk. Beginning like I do every morning, I spent some time in His Word. He said, "Do not 'grow weary and lose heart.' Run with perseverance. Run the race I have marked out for you." My reply? "Yes, Lord. One yes at a time!"

Please don't let comparison interfere with running the race God has marked out for you. You may not be the swiftest, the smoothest, or the sleekest, but you have as much right to run as anyone else who pays the dues. You may not finish first or second—you might even bring up the rear like I did—but no matter. Fix your eyes on Jesus and keep running. Even if you have to crawl across the finish line, if God has given you a dream, don't let comparison hinder you. Step up, compete, and let God be the judge of where you place when you cross the finish line.

16

DOUBT

❧❧

I've always believed in listening for his voice,
but I've generally found that listening to God
is indistinct work. You never know if it's really God or
if it is your own stumblebum alter ego.[1]

CALVIN MILLER

You don't seriously believe God made the world in six days do you?"
he said, staring at me open-mouthed. "And all that stuff about
Noah and every type of animal in the world on *one* boat? That's ridicu-
lous! Jonah, swallowed by a fish and coughed up on some foreign shore
days later? Absolutely ludicrous. I thought you were smarter than that,"
he remarked with disgust before turning and walking out of my life forever. You've probably had conversations like this one that I had with a
friend on a university campus after he read a brief testimonial of my
decision to follow Christ in a campus flyer. He came looking for me,
convinced that there must be two Connie Cavanaughs on campus, and
it must be the *other* one who was mouthing such claptrap.

I had no answers that would have satisfied him that day. More than
30 years later, I probably still don't. I asked Jesus to come into my life
on faith, not on empirical fact. My friend wanted me to prove the miracles listed in Scripture to convince him the gospel was worthy of his
consideration. But even Jesus knew people couldn't recognize Him as
God unless God revealed His divinity to them.[2]

People have devoted their lives to trying to prove the claims of

Scripture. You can read their books, visit their websites, accompany them on archeological digs, and attend their seminars if you care to. While I find their work fascinating, that pursuit has never been part of the race marked out for me.[3] "We walk by faith, not by sight," Paul says.[4] In this case "walk" means our "way of life," how we act, our behavior.[5] So this verse, in a broader sense, means our actions are guided by the God we can't see but whom we trust to lead us every step of the way. To walk by faith is to follow God one yes at a time.

All of us decide, consciously or subconsciously, where to place our faith. We either believe God created life or we assume life began a different way. Both require faith. The leap of faith needed to bridge the gigantic gaps in evolutionary theory is no different than that needed to believe that Jesus turned water into wine, walked on waves, and raised the dead. I've placed my faith in the Creator God and His messianic Son, Jesus Christ. Many people, unhappy with both those options, refuse to think about it. They say, "I'll deal with the 'origin of life' question just before I die. Right now I just want to live!"

The problem is that many of us don't get a memo letting us know when the end is near. Some of us die without warning. That means we don't always have a chance to "get back to the issue" of whether to believe in God and accept Jesus' sacrifice for our salvation. These folks strap on spiritual blinders and throw themselves into whatever earthly pursuits grab their fancy, denying they have a need for God and never looking up until tragedy strikes. Then it may or may not be too late to think about the big questions of life. I don't say this to scare you or intimidate you into making a hasty decision. It's just a reality of our existence. We all die. And then what?

Have you put as much thought into your eternal future as you have your retirement? Perhaps you've obtained your "key" to the Pearly Gates by accepting Jesus as your Savior but, like so many church attendees, that's as far as you've gotten. You haven't really learned to follow God in your daily life. The biggest barrier holding you back is doubt. You *want* to believe, you *do* believe, but you are plagued by doubt. Like the man who brought his son to Jesus for healing after the disciples failed, are you saying to God, "I do believe! Help my unbelief."[6]

Doubt Lurks in the Church

Doubt that God is who the Bible says He is and that He has done what the Bible records is a barrier some people never get past. They don't place their lives in God's capable, loving hands. But an insidious reality is that many people warming seats in our churches on Sunday mornings are plagued with doubts. They doubt the truth of the Bible, they doubt God is concerned with them personally, they doubt God is love because there's too much suffering in the world. They doubt God still works miracles because they haven't seen any. Their doubts form a swampland that bogs them down as they try to follow God.

Brenda's Story

Brenda, a reader of my work and a fellow wilderness wanderer, emailed me: "I know how to talk the talk and to look like I'm walking the walk (done it a long time), but I live with a lot of doubts and fears and just no real joy in the Lord."[7] She went on, "Sometimes I feel like I've lived in the doubts for so long that I really wouldn't know how 'not' to live in them. And maybe that's just the way it's going to be." Brenda's plaintive heart cry is one I've heard repeatedly in response to talking and writing about spiritual dryness.

Brenda's journey into wilderness began in earnest about 13 years ago, when she lost her little six-year-old daughter. Brenda's child was born just months after Brenda lost her mom to cancer. The girl was born with a fatal disorder. They knew from the beginning that her life would be short, and that meant "several years of grief even before her death." Not long after she died, Brenda's daddy, with whom she had deeply bonded during her grief, also passed away. Loss upon loss took their toll. "Loneliness, emptiness, some depression, [inability to] find my place and expecting my husband to meet those needs" drove Brenda and her husband to the brink of divorce. They were "able to work things out" and stay together. After attending church as a couple for more than 15 years, Brenda's spouse dropped out. He says he'll never go back.

Feeling Like a Fake

Brenda continued to share:

I know I've not allowed God to take control of my life. I don't know how. I feel so unworthy if I'm in a group and we're going around the room and each one is to pray. I feel like just a "fake." I struggle with reading my Bible, which I know doesn't help my faith. And then I am so saddened and embarrassed by my prayer life. I don't have that open communication with Him like I should. I feel so distant from Him a lot, and I don't really know how to talk to Him. I just want to move on with life. I feel like I just go along trying to do the best I can but still living with the doubts and feelings of unworthiness.

When you go through things, aren't you supposed to become better? Don't we go through them to be able to help someone else? I've just been left numb, and I feel I've really disappointed God because I don't have that joy inside. One of the saddest things I deal with is that I don't have the joy or excitement in my life that I should to show others how good God is or express what all He has done for me (and deep down I know He truly has taken care of me and blessed my life), to even "sell" my family members [on Jesus].

Brenda thanked me for listening and apologized for the lengthy email.

Interlocking Barriers

Brenda's email clearly shows the overlapping emotions of guilt and shame that her doubt has elicited. Most of us face many interlocking barriers in our quest to follow God. The good news is that if one barrier begets another, then often one solution also leads to another. Cutting through the barrier of fear helps us make great strides against comparison. Overcoming doubt improves our standing regarding guilt and shame.

If you see you have many barriers to overcome, my best advice is to simply *follow God one yes at a time*. Let Him lead you away from the brink and through the barriers one at a time. Overcoming one barrier brings positive gains against other hindrances because of their inter-connectedness.

Brenda isn't alone in her struggle. Have you ever read the *Complete Idiot's Guide to the Bible* (I wonder if this is a guide for complete idiots or a comprehensive book)? It says, "Sometimes God will seem distant—perhaps so distant that we will wonder if we only imagined his existence when he felt so close."[8] Brenda said, "I guess I could just use a little push to get going in the right direction again." Brenda's words became a challenge for me to put into words a message of hope for those who struggle with doubt. The little push Brenda craves is created when we look to God to provide the opportunity to say the first yes and then follow that by saying yes, and continuing to do so. Every *simple, immediate, possible* yes is a nudge on the rudder of our lives that eventually can change our direction. The tricky part is how do we, as doubters, find the faith to say the first yes?

The Doubt Swamp

"To doubt" is "to be undecided or skeptical about; to regard as unlikely."[9] As a noun, "doubt" is the "lack of certainty that often leads to irresolution." This definition is why I characterize the barrier of doubt as a swamp we can get bogged down in, unable to move forward in faith. Doubt can also be called "a lack of trust." This is the bull's eye definition because doubt belies the very title "believer." To believe is to trust. To doubt is unbelief. To be caught in the murky swamp of doubt is to be unsettled or unresolved. Doubt feels unsettling, doesn't it?

Sometimes as we follow the dreams God plants in our hearts, our faith withers and we stumble into the swamp of doubt (unbelief). That's what happened to Dennis, an army chaplain, pastor, and son of a pastor.

Dennis' Story

Alone in my room in the barracks, I had slipped to the very bottom. I never thought that it was possible but I am sure the prodigal son felt the same. I knew that was it; either I turn back to God or walk away from Him. It was a scary place to be. The real struggle was my concern that I had lost my way and God would not take me back. Even though I believed *once saved always saved* I was not sure anymore.[10]

That night was the culmination of seven years of spiritual drought for Dennis. He describes that season as a time of "no joy, just sorrows; no fun, just labor; no victory, just defeats." Meanwhile he was preaching about running the race and living in Christ, but personally he felt beaten. "The race I was running was more of a crawl. I had lost all sense of direction. I felt alone and hopeless." In the midst of his wilderness he still sensed God's call had been genuine, going back to his own "rock" experience from time to time. But he felt so powerless and abandoned. His faith had shrunk to a mere speck.

During his dry season Dennis got three tattoos. One was designed by his son. It's a cross, an anchor, a banner that reads "Bydand" (Gaelic for "Stand Fast"), and 2 Corinthians 10:4.[11] This helped remind Dennis of God's love and provision and got him moving forward again. Having left the pastorate and gone back into the army, Dennis wondered if he would be given another chance to lead a church. After coming out of the wilderness, he wanted to share what he had learned with others: "Only God can make a way in the wilderness. Only He can destroy the strongholds or fortresses. Only He can gain us the victory. Our role is to be faithful and open to His leading, willing to join Him where He shows us."

The last time I ran into Dennis, he was well on his way. He no longer looked defeated; he was more like the man I'd met many years earlier. He was filled with renewed hope and promise. Now the pastor of an English-speaking Chinese congregation of young families, Dennis' faith and life are moving forward again. Starting from that lowest-of-low points in the hotel room where he said "yes" to God once again, Dennis has seen his faith grow again as he uses his wilderness experience to transform and strengthen his present ministry.

Take Doubts to God

God invites His children to come straight to Him with their doubts. Over and over the psalmists called out to God in transparent honesty:

"Lord, how long will You continually forget me? How long will You hide Your face from me? How long will I store up anxious concerns within me, agony in my mind every day?"[12] Can you relate? Me too! Yet we feel so guilty about doubting that we stay in the swamp, mired, refusing to humble ourselves and get beyond our feelings to talk to God and accept His help and comfort. Robert B. Chisholm, in his commentary on the book of Lamentations, writes:

> Lamentations…shows the honest face of prayer in the midst of tragedy. It frees God's people to question and still experience His presence. It shows that the road to hope is paved with honesty and questioning, mixed with praise. Faith grows in the midst of crisis when God's people take their troubles to Him.[13]

God invites us to come to Him with our troubles, our questions, our fears—and our doubts and guilt. Jesus' loving treatment of "Doubting" Thomas when He invites him to "put your finger here and observe My hands. Reach out your hand and put it into My side. Don't be an unbeliever, but a believer"[14] beautifully illustrates His loving understanding of our penchant to doubt unless we see verifiable proof.

The Vital Ingredient

Everybody follows somebody or something. Even leaders are followers. Whether you follow a person or your own set of personal principles, there is something absolutely vital involved in the relationship: trust. We follow people or ideas we believe are trustworthy. Sometimes the ones we trust and choose to follow prove to be untrustworthy and we get burned, but the reason we fell in line in the first place was because of trust.

Brenda's story is a classic example of how believers move from vibrant faith to debilitating doubt. The death of her daughter caused her to question God's love and provision. Similar to Brenda's, my *doubt* that led to my wilderness experience was also born of suffering and then fed by *fear*. Once I was "in deep," *guilt* and *shame* took over, making it extremely difficult to even contemplate escaping the swamp of despair. When God found me and began to lead me out *one yes at a time, comparison* raised its ugly head and tried to hold me back. But just as surely as faith is a spiritual gift, so "little faith" is a common but not fatal condition.[15] The disciples were diagnosed with little faith on several occasions, and yet those same disciples went on to live courageous lives and many died as martyrs, unwavering in their faith.[16] Does that mean there's hope for people today who battle doubt?

How Much Faith Is Enough?

Let's revisit the story of the man who wanted help with his unbelief. While Jesus was "up on a high mountain" with Peter, James and John, His other disciples were in a big flap with Jewish scribes that drew a curious crowd.[17] Coming down from the mountain, Jesus approached the group and asked what they were arguing about. A man from the crowd explained that he had brought his son who suffered from seizures to the disciples for healing, but they were unable to do it. Jesus asked to see the boy. The lad was brought forth, at which point he fell into convulsions at Jesus' feet. Jesus asked the father how long this had been going on. "'From childhood,' he said. 'And many times it has thrown him into fire or water to destroy him. But if you can do anything, have compassion on us and help us.'"[18]

What a heartbreaking scene. What a desperate heart cry. To more fully understand the head and heart of the father of this afflicted child, listen to the story of a man whose son suffers today:

> I have a son named Joshua. Joshua was born healthy, but became disabled early in life due to the toxic effects of a childhood vaccine. For years I held the belief his disability was unacceptable. I experienced significant hurt, anger, and fear. I spent the first five years of Joshua's life in a state of war. I was angry at the world. I lashed out at others. I was miserable. I ached for peace, but the possibility felt far, far away. I believed I could experience peace and joy only if my son's condition improved. In the meantime, I felt powerless.[19]

Ted Kuntz's son is permanently mentally disabled, racked with seizures more than a dozen times a day, confined to a wheelchair, and in need of constant assistance all because of a reaction to a vaccine at five months of age. By the time he was five, the medical community had done all they knew to do and admitted defeat. The Children's Hospital informed them they would no longer treat Joshua because there was nothing they could do to improve his condition. Ted wrote:

> Words cannot express the pain I felt. I loathed watching my son seize over and over…I lived in a state of constant dread…Waking each morning, knowing I was to face another day of seizing, tears, and helplessness, became an unbearable struggle. Thoughts of suicide visited me frequently. This caused even more guilt and pain. I hated my life. I felt trapped. I felt hopeless. I doubted I would ever be happy again.[20]

Can You Help Us?

Imagine what hope the biblical father of the seizure-prone son had when he took his son to the disciples of the Miracle Worker. Maybe the Nazarene had shared some of His power with them? Or maybe Jesus Himself would be there to heal his son. Now feel his pain when the disciples couldn't heal the boy. Was that hard to do? Or have you had your hopes dashed before? That sickening plunge as the bottom falls out invites despair, doesn't it? The father of the boy must have been utterly stricken. His recent disappointment fuels his desperate plea when Jesus shows up: "But *if You can* do anything, have compassion on us and help us," the dad asks Jesus.

And how did Jesus respond to the father? "'If You can?' Everything is possible to the one who believes."[21] How would you react to a statement like Jesus'? If everything is possible to one who believes, then why weren't the disciples able to heal the boy? Didn't they believe? The Scripture doesn't indicate whether that even crossed the father's mind. Instead of blaming them, he assumes the guilt and says these infamous words, the words that have become the Doubter's Prayer as he struggles to make headway in the gluey swamp: "I do believe! Help my unbelief."[22]

The father is saying he does have *some* faith, but not much. And possibly not enough to bring healing to his boy whom he loves more than life itself. His answer betrays our thinking even today that faith is a thing we hold in quantity. Some people (usually others and seldom us) seem to have lots of faith—all they need with plenty left over. But you and me? Sometimes it seems we hardly have any at all. How do we decide this? Because just like this father, we come to situations in life that seem to depend on faith and we fall short. Our faith doesn't measure up. We are like the kid who grows so slowly that year after year he fails to meet the height standard for the roller coaster at the amusement park and has to go back to the twirling teacups in shame.

Faith Is Not a Noun

Faith is not a person, place, or thing. It's not a noun. It's a verb—an action. It's not something *we have* but something *we do*. Everybody starts out with the same "amount" of faith, which is the size of a mustard seed.[23] And it never really grows bigger. It doesn't have to because mustard-seed faith is big enough to move mountains! It doesn't get bigger, but it does get stronger. Faith that is exercised can do more.

Our churches are filled with people who are like the father of the epileptic boy—people who *do* believe but who need help with their unbelief. They doubt some of those same claims in the Bible that my college friend was aghast about when he found out I believed them. Guilt and shame keep believers silent because Christ-followers are "supposed to" believe the whole Bible, talking donkeys and all.[24] They feel like second-class Christians because they can't explain to unbelievers the miraculous biblical accounts of walls tumbling, bones connecting, and flaming chariots ascending.[25] So what they do instead is avoid Bible discussions of any kind to circumvent the embarrassment of admitting their unbelief. Like the disciples, they have "little faith," and they feel like it's not enough to accomplish great things for God.

What we need to realize is that every great thing is accomplished *one yes at a time*. So how much faith do we really need? Only enough for the next *simple, immediate, possible* yes. We can carry our problem to God just like the father brought his ailing son to Jesus. We can explain to Jesus how long the problem has been threatening to destroy us. We can ask Him for help, even admitting that we aren't even sure *if* He can help. We can say out loud that we "sorta" believe and admit we are plagued by doubt. We can ask Him to help our unbelief. Then we can ask Him to show us the next *simple, immediate, possible yes* and to give us the strength and courage to say yes with our feet. We *do* faith. We take one tiny step forward. Like any journey, faith starts with one step.

FOLLOW-SHIP

So what does it look like to follow God one yes at a time? Even though the principles are the same, the pathway is different for each of us. All of us have our stories, our journeys, our barriers to overcome. I get a lot of feedback from people after they hear me talk about following God one yes at a time. Alana's email captures the message perfectly and will implant a picture in your mind that accurately depicts what this life of "follow-ship" looks like. It is her gift to me and to you:

Connie,

I attended the retreat last weekend where you spoke, and I just wanted to share with you what God showed me. I came to the camp dragging my heels. You see, I saw what the topic for the weekend was [Following God One Yes at a Time], and it was no mystery what God wanted to say to me. I had already been asked by Him to do something. But this was no *little* door that He wanted me to walk through. To me it looked like a giant wall. And I had scaled that wall about halfway and then got stuck. And that's where I've been for the past two months. Not willing to continue saying "yes" and paralyzed by fear. I knew that is what I would be confronting this weekend, but I had no idea *how* God was going to be able to move me because I honestly did not want to move. What He was asking me to do was simply too hard.

Anyway, on Friday night when I arrived at the camp and it came time to sign up for activities, I signed up to do the High Ropes Course. I honestly don't know what I was thinking. Some friends that I came with were going to do it and seemed excited about it so I thought, *Why not?* It sounded like fun, and I'm always up for a physical challenge. The next afternoon at the appointed time and when I got to the top of that first tree, I realized that yes, the course would be physically challenging, but fun? Not so much. It was actually quite terrifying. You see, I knew in my head that I could not fall; I was tethered with two lanyards to a super-strong cable. However, I was being asked to step, climb, balance, and reach on ropes and boards suspended 20 to 30 feet in the air. Never mind that I couldn't fall! It was scary!

The only reason I stepped onto the course was because, in all honesty, I was too full of pride to climb back down and quit. I made it to the second-last portion of this six-leg high-ropes course before trouble hit. This particular section was made up of eight or so long, narrow boards put end-to-end and suspended by ropes along the sides. I stepped off the platform and onto the first board and, hanging onto the ropes, I went from board to board. And then I got to the middle where, as my friends on the ground were warning me, there was a big gap. Sure enough, the gap between the next two planks was so large that I could not simply *step* to the next board; I was going to have to jump. I froze.

There was no way I was going to let go of the ropes and jump while holding onto nothing—do I have to remind you that I am 30 feet off the ground? So now I was ready to quit, asking if they could get me down from here. Well, my friends turned their support up a notch and encouraged me and tried to help me along. What ended up happening is they sent the girl who was coming up behind me to my rescue. When she stepped onto the board that I was frozen to, it pushed the board forward enough that the gap closed and I was able to step to the next board. I became *unstuck* and was able to finish the rest of the course and, thankfully, get my feet back on solid ground (where I like them and will be keeping them, thank-you-very-much!).

Sure enough, God started speaking very clearly to me on Sunday morning with the story about the disciples in the boat and the storm. [The message was based on Matthew 14, when Jesus sends His disciples across the Sea of Galilee ahead of Him, and they get caught in a storm halfway across the lake. I referred to this storm as a potential quitting point and said that to follow Jesus the disciples needed to keep rowing.] I started to see the parallels between that story and my own life. Saying "yes" to God was getting hard and I found myself in a storm. And I had given up, stopped paddling, and frozen up just like I did on the ropes course. I realized that I was paralyzed by fear. My fear was a barrier that was keeping me from following God by saying yes to what I knew He wanted me to do. I knew that taking the next step would mean facing some things in my life that I had buried deep, deep down, and I didn't want to face them. God showed me that morning that no matter how scared I was *I could not fall.* He has me tightly in His grasp. And He will walk through this next "yes" with me. *And* He sent along friends and family to pray for me and to encourage me.

So God used this weekend to unstick me. As I write this to you I am contemplating how to take the next step. You see, the wall I am facing is Depression and Anxiety. The first few steps that I took were fairly easy: get medicated, start exercising, do light therapy, etc. Now that my mood is stable, the next step is to go to counseling to address the root causes. This is what I fear the most—having to dig up past hurts and dealing with them, especially now that I'm feeling better. But I suspect God wants more for me than to just feel better. He wants to heal me. And I have to do this as a part of the healing.

If you think of me, would you pray for me? I'm hoping the next set of steps (finding an affordable, Christian counselor whom I "click" with) goes fairly smoothly because I'm not sure I can handle much more than that at this point. Anyway, thank you so much for sharing so openly about your life and letting God use you.

In Him,
Alana

Alana's frank telling of her experience on the high ropes course and the ensuing personalized message from God is a beautiful illustration of how God works in our lives as we follow Him one yes at a time. Some yeses are easier than others. Some yeses look so treacherous that, like Alana, we might freeze up and get stuck for a while. Sometimes we get so stuck that God sends "angels" in the form of friends or even complete strangers to steady things and give us the courage to "go for it." The reality is that *God wants us* to follow Him so He does whatever it takes to clearly reveal the next step to us and then helps us find the resources within ourselves or from the outside to say yes and take that step of faith. And when we risk it, say yes, and step out, He announces to the angels and saints gathered around His heavenly throne, "This is My beloved child in whom I am well pleased."

If I had never said yes to God, I would still be barricaded behind my fear, unaware that on the other side of that self-made wall was a life of adventure, personal growth, renewed faith, and rewarding service. If Elva-Jean and Leon had never said yes to God, they would have wasted their suffering, trashed their marriage and destroyed their family. Instead they found a deeper love and respect for one another, as well as a new arena of ministry to hurting couples. If Agnes had not said yes she would have missed the soul-freedom that forgiveness brings and the opportunity to share healing love with her son-in-law, the father and only living parent of the grandchildren she is raising.

What is your story? Does your life feel like a high ropes course? Does it seem like walking this path of obedience God has set is a lot riskier and scarier than you imagined it would be? Like me, you may have deluded yourself into thinking that walking with Jesus would eventually lead you to a life of tranquil circumstances, smooth roads, and calm waters. Not so, fellow paddler! Following Jesus can feel downright dangerous and terrifying. So much so that we often forget that we can't fall. In other words, God holds our lives in His capable hands, and even if our earthly lives should suddenly end, we are immediately scooped into His forever presence.

If you find yourself stuck along the pathway of following Him— too scared to move forward, unable to go back—call out to Jesus. He *will* send help. Don't expect an airlift, but look for Him to steady you and encourage you. Then take a deep breath…and say yes!

NOTES

Chapter 1: The Dream

1. Exodus 3:10.
2. Exodus 3:12.
3. Exodus 4:12.
4. John 10:27-28.
5. Genesis 15:5; 22:17; 13:16.
6. Exodus 3:8.
7. 1 Chronicles 28:9.

Chapter 2: Simple

1. Billy Graham, *How to Be Born Again* (Nashville: Thomas Nelson, 1989), p. 53.
2. Metis: a person of mixed parentage: typically French or Scottish and Canadian First Nation's People.
3. Bannock: A thick, flat cakey bread made of flour, water, baking powder, fat and salt that can be baked in an oven, cooked on a griddle, deep fried in hot oil, or roasted over a fire. Oven-cooked bannock is a staple in most Metis and First Nations' homes in Canada.
4. Thom S. Rainer and Art Rainer, *Simple Life* (Nashville: B&H Publishing Group and Lifeway Research, 2009), p. 8.
5. Genesis 12:1.
6. Genesis 25:8.
7. Genesis 12:2-3.
8. Genesis 17:17.
9. Hebrews 11:8.
10. Exodus 3:10.
11. Exodus 2:11-15.
12. Exodus 3:11.
13. Exodus 3:12.
14. Exodus 3:13–4:13.
15. Psalm 119:105.

Chapter 3: Immediate

1. Genesis 22:13.
2. Wallace Immen, "When a Challenge Seems Too Big," *Globe and Mail* (Canada's national business newspaper), Friday, June 4, 2010, p. B15.
3. Ibid.
4. Ibid.

Chapter 4: Possible

1. Matthew 14:22.
2. Matthew 14:24.
3. Ibid.
4. Henry Blackaby, *Unlimiting God* (Colorado Springs: Multnomah Books, 2008), p. 125.
5. Matthew 14:27,32.
6. Immen, "When a Challenge Seems Too Big," p. B15.
7. Sarah Hampson, "Keep on Rolling," *The Globe and Mail* (Canadian national business newspaper), Friday, March 19, 2010, p. L2.
8. Ibid.
9. Matthew 19:26.

Chapter 5: God Speaks

1. Henry Blackaby and Richard Blackaby, *Hearing God's Voice* (Nashville: Broadman and Holman Publishers, 2002), p. 17.
2. "I will watch to see what God is doing around me and join Him," in Henry Blackaby, Richard Blackaby, Claude King, *Experiencing God,* rev. and exp. (Nashville: Lifeway, 2007), p. 34.
3. Matthew 18:10-14.
4. Robert Pritikin, *The Pritikin Weight Loss Breakthrough* (New York: Dutton, 1998).
5. Rainer and Rainer, *Simple Life,* p. 50.
6. Blackaby and Blackaby, *Hearing God's Voice*, p. 187.
7. Psalm 51:13 NIV.
8. Matthew 18:10-14.
9. Exodus 3:1-4.
10. Exodus 3:10.
11. Exodus 4:12-16.
12. Joshua 1:5.

Chapter 6: Chocolates

1. Bill Hybels, *Just Walk Across the Room* (Grand Rapids, MI: Zondervan, 2006), p. 86.
2. John H. Sammis (1846–1919), "Trust and Obey."
3. Judges 6:12.
4. Gideon was threshing wheat in a wine vat to hide it from the marauding Midianites (Judges 6:11). In Old Testament times the presses for making wine were usually cut or hewed out of rock and

connected by channels to lower rock-cut vats where the juice was allowed to collect and ferment [Chad Brand, Charles Draper, Archie England, gen. eds., *Holman Illustrated Bible Dictionary* (Nashville: Holman Bible Publishers, 2003), p. 1675.]

5. Judges 6:13.
6. Judges 6:14.
7. Judges 6:15.
8. Judges 6:16.
9. Judges 6:17.
10. Judges 6:25-26.
11. Judges 6:27-30.
12. Judges 7:12.
13. Judges 7:2.
14. Judges 7:18.

Chapter 7: Peace

1. James Stuart Bell and Stan Campbell, *The Complete Idiot's Guide to the Bible,* 3rd ed. (New York: Alpha, 2005), p. 386.
2. See www.gnolive.ca for more information.
3. 2 Corinthians 12:7.
4. 2 Corinthians 12:8-9.
5. 2 Corinthians 12:9-10.
6. Philippians 4:7 NIV.
7. Ibid.

Chapter 8: Power

1. David R. Beck, contributor, in Brand, Draper, England, gen. eds., *Holman Illustrated Bible Dictionary*, p. 1501.
2. Exodus 14:29.
3. Brand, Draper, England, gen. eds., *Holman Illustrated Bible Dictionary*, p. 1501.
4. Ibid., p. 1502.
5. John 6:26; Matthew 12:39.
6. John 2:11.
7. John 14:6,12-18.
8. Genesis 22:13.
9. Matthew 7:7-8.
10. Philippians 3:14.
11. Philippians 3:10.

Chapter 9: Provision

1. Aron Ralston, *Between a Rock and a Hard Place* (New York: Atria Books, 2004).

2. Ibid., p. 321.

3. Ibid., p. 342.

4. Tom Elliff, *The Red Feather* (Oklahoma City: Living in the Word Publications, 2008), p. 90.

5. Ibid., p. 94.

6. Ibid.

7. To hear Cesar Parra give a brief overview of the Action 52 evangelism plan go to http://www.e-quip.net/presentations/show/2188.

8. Isaiah 55:8.

9. Jeremiah 31:3.

10. Romans 5:8.

Chapter 10: Presence

1. Marshall Broomhall, *The Man Who Believed God* (Edinburgh, Scotland: R&R Clark Ltd., 1930), p. 174. These words were spoken during a message he gave at a missionary conference in Shanghai, 1889.

2. This letter has been modified from the original for readability. "Taryn" was used to protect the letter writer's privacy.

3. Ibid.

4. Brennan Manning, *The Relentless Tenderness of Jesus* (Grand Rapids, MI: Fleming H. Revell, 2004), pp. 9-10.

5. Ibid., p. 9.

6. Ibid., p. 10.

7. Luke 3:22.

8. Charles Trumbull, *The Life That Wins* (Fort Washington, PN: Christian Literature Crusade, 1971), pp. 20-21.

9. Pastor Dwayne Bartley, from my notes taken at an evangelism workshop he led at the Canadian National Baptist Convention in Ottawa, Ontario, Canada, July 2007. Used by permission.

Chapter 11: Fear

1. Ted Kuntz, MEd, *Peace Begins with Me* (Coquitlam, BC: Ted Kuntz, 2005), p. 39.

2. Ibid.

3. Elva-Jean Brown's story as submitted to me via email with some edits. Used with permission from Elva-Jean and Leon Brown, July 2010.

4. Church planting: starting a new church with a few people, limited funds, and typically in a home or rental facility.

5. Grace Fox, *Moving from Fear to Freedom: A Woman's Guide to Peace in Every Situation* (Eugene, OR: Harvest House Publishers, 2007), p. 11.

6. Ibid.

7. Kathy Howard, *Before His Throne: Discovering the Wonder of Intimacy with a Holy God* (Birmingham, AL: New Hope Publishers, 2008), p. 9.

8. Ibid., p. 19.

9. Matthew 14:30.

10. Matthew 14:31.

11. Joshua 6:20.

Chapter 12: Pride

1. Larry Hein, quoted in Manning, *Relentless Tenderness of Jesus*, p. 29.

2. Philippians 2:3.

3. Philippians 2:8.

4. 1 Peter 5:5.

5. 1 Peter 5:6.

6. Exodus 34:33.

Chapter 13: Guilt

1. Ten more years passed before I finally followed God one yes at a time and confessed everything to Joan. She gave full and complete absolution. Obviously the barrier of pride was alive and well for a long time.

2. David D. Burns, MD, *Feeling Good: The New Mood Therapy* (New York: Quill, 2000), p. 199.

3. Ephesians 2:8-9.

4. "Therefore if anyone is in Christ, there is a new creation; old things have passed away, and look, new things have come"(2 Corinthians 5: 17).

5. Romans 8:35-39.

Chapter 14: Shame

1. David S. Dockery, gen. ed., *Holman Concise Bible Commentary* (Nashville: Broadman & Holman Publishers, 1998), p. 547.

2. Alcoholics Anonymous, *Big Book*, 4th ed. (New York: A.A. World Services Inc., 2001), p. 72.

Chapter 15: Comparison

1. Story told by Jim Messner. Used by permission.

2. Chris Thurman, PhD, *The Lies We Tell Ourselves* (Nashville: Thomas Nelson, 1999), p. iv.

3. Philippians 3:8-14.

Chapter 16: Doubt

1. Calvin Miller, *Life Is Mostly Edges* (Nashville: Thomas Nelson, 2008), p. 261.

2. Matthew 16:17.

3. Hebrews 12:1.

4. 2 Corinthians 5:7.

5. Bullet notes, Holman Christian Standard Bible (Nashville: Holman Bible Publishers, 2005), sv 2 Corinthians 5:7.

6. Mark 9:24.

7. This personal story was emailed to me. I've changed the names and some details to protect the privacy of the people invovled.

8. Bell and Campbell, *Complete Idiot's Guide*, p. 389.

9. The American Heritage Dictionary of the English Language, 4th ed (Orlando: Houghton Mifflin Co., 2009), sv "doubt." All rights reserved.

10. Personal conversation with Dennis Milne, 2010. Used by permission.

11. "Although we are walking in the flesh, we do not wage war in a fleshly way, since the weapons of our warfare are not fleshly, but are powerful through God for the demolition of strongholds" (2 Corinthians 10:3-4).

12. Psalm 13:1-2.

13. Robert B. Chisholm, *"The Major Prophets,"* in Dockery, gen. ed., *Holman Concise Bible Commentary*, p. 313.

14. John 20:27.

15. 1 Corinthians 12:7-9; Matthew 14:31.

16. Matthew 6:30; 8:26; 14:31; 16:8; 17:20; Luke 12:28.

17. Mark 9:14.

18. Mark 9:21-22.

19. Kuntz, *Peace Begins with Me,* p. 19.

20. Ibid., pp. 218-19.

21. Mark 9:23.

22. Mark 9:24.

23. Matthew 17:20.

24. Numbers 22:28.

25. Joshua 7:20; Ezekiel 37:7; 2 Kings 2:11.

Acknowledgments

My heartfelt thanks to *each brave soul whose story is told herein*. Your honesty will give people renewed hope as they discover how to follow God one yes at a time.

To Gerry. Your fingerprints are on every page. Our ongoing dialogue became the ramp by which I snuck into your brain, plundered shamelessly, and then scurried back to my desk to jot it all down and claim it as my own.

To my children. Christine and Anita, thank you for your friendship, unconditional love, rich grace, and three perfect grandkids. *JP*, I love your tender heart and that you end every visit and call with "I love you." My Louisiana sons, *Brad and Kyle*, you are so easy to love! Grammy hugs and kisses to *Jasmine, Eli*, and *Madi*.

To the *"anonymous one"* whose daily prayers fly through blue glass—you give me wings to share God's love.

Kathy Howard, thank you for running the "writer" race with me and encouraging me every step of the way.

Sue Rainey, your tender care, wisdom, and belief in me helped immensely. Thank you.

Carolyn Curtis, thank you for your for seasoned guidance, positive critiques, and abundant praise.

Karen Willoughby, you are a treasure who keeps on giving, but you live too far away.

Shannon Luyendyck—artist, cowgirl, and gym buddy. I'm indebted…and stiff.

To *Terry Glaspey* for believing in the message, and to my editor, *Barb Gordon*, for making it so much better. Thank you.

So many others should be mentioned, and if you, *my friend*, are one of them, let me know and I'll buy lunch!

"So, what's God been doing in your life lately?"

If you cringe when you hear that question, you're not alone.

Almost every believer experiences periods of spiritual dryness or disconnectedness from God. Right now, you may be one of them.

*Truth is, you haven't lost your faith…
you're simply finding your own faith.*

It's okay to become disillusioned with God and Christianity *as you now know them*, says author Connie Cavanaugh. Out of her own life experience, she urges you to keep asking, seeking, and knocking. Then you will move away from the desert and toward a fresh realization—deeper and more mature—of friendship with God as He truly is.

Hold on to hope—He's calling you back.

You'll never find the peace you're looking for if you drop out. Instead, be honest about where you are and get ready to listen to the Father, who's never stopped loving you. You'll begin to see life springing up in dry places…and you'll move from faking it to finding grace from the God who was there all along.

*"This profoundly relevant and life-changing book will move you,
convict you, and encourage and bless you. I urge you to read it."*

RICHARD BLACKABY, COAUTHOR,
Experiencing God Day by Day